Understanding
effective learning

Understanding effective learning

Strategies for the classroom

Des Hewitt

 Open University Press

Open University Press
McGraw-Hill Education
McGraw-Hill House
Shoppenhangers Road
Maidenhead
Berkshire
England
SL6 2QL

email: enquiries@openup.co.uk
world wide web: www.openup.co.uk

and Two Penn Plaza, New York, NY 10121-2289, USA

First published 2008

A catalogue record of this book is available from the British Library

ISBN-13: 978 0 335 222377 (pb) 13: 978 0 335 222360 (hb)
ISBN-10: 0 335 222374 (pb) 10: 0 335 222366 (hb)

Library of Congress Cataloging-in-Publication Data
CIP data applied for

Typeset by RefineCatch Limited, Bungay, Suffolk
Printed in Great Britain by Bell and Bain Ltd, Glasgow

The **McGraw·Hill** Companies

Contents

Acknowledgements

Writing a book can be daunting proposition, but many people have made this much easier than I thought it could have been.

Colleagues at the University of Derby have been particularly supportive. Professor Marie Parker-Jenkins encouraged me every step of the way for this book and others. John Dolan has provided an insightful view of my research as the foundations for this book were set.

I would like to thank all the students I have ever worked with at Derby in the University and in local schools. They have provided me with the inspiration for this book and a huge amount of enjoyment in nearly every lesson I have ever taught.

It gives me great pleasure that my parents, Ken and Marie, were able to read this book before they passed away. I must thank them for the constantly positive voice which drives everything I do.

Finally, I would like to dedicate this book to my wife Shirley and children, Lucy, Nanette and Daniel. I promise the next book will have more pictures in it!

Foreword

The underachievement of groups of learners remains of paramount concern in contemporary society. 'Understanding Effective Learning: Strategies for the Classroom' is a welcome addition to the debate and indicates the way forward. In a scholarly yet accessible way, this book challenges us to think specifically about school processes and strategies to bring about effective learning. Importantly, this publication focuses on the needs of the individual learner, a refreshing reminder that we should place the child at the centre of the learning process – a view that has been lost considerably since the introduction of the English National Curriculum (1989).

Dr Hewitt's research on classroom practice began in the early 1990's when he embarked on an in-depth qualitative study of pupils' perceptions of learning and the strategies they use as autonomous learners. This book is the product of that initial inquiry and has broadened out to include whole school approaches to using learning strategies. Through a number of well-conceived chapters, the publication begins with an overview of the concept of learning, and models of instruction. Subsequent chapters explore the themes of: problems with learning; social settings within education; and developing learning strategies with regard to both the individual learner and the teacher. Finally the publication draws together key arguments concerning recent debates about 'standards' and effective learning. A glossary provides definition of the key terms, and activities for educationalists to reflect on their own practice.

In today's climate of raising academic achievement, launched by the Government 'Aiming High' agenda (DfES 2003), this is a timely publication. It is underpinned by scholarship, building on the work of Vygotsky, Pollard, and Claxton, and the book makes a welcome contribution to the field. Dr Hewitt bases his work on the view that

> a person may be socialised into the norms of an organisation without being aware of the learning or what the norms are
>
> (Eraut 2000, p. 18).

'Understanding Effective Learning: Strategies for the Classroom' works to ensure that teachers, trainees and schools do not forget this maxim. Through the theoretical and practical advice contained in this book educationalists can have a greater awareness of the learning process and significantly improve pupil achievement.

Marie Parker-Jenkins
Professor of Research in Education
University of Derby
2008

Introduction

A person may be socialised into the norms of an organisation without being aware either of the learning or of what the norms are.

(Eraut 2000: 118)

This chapter will help you to:

- understand the concept of learning strategies and why they are important for children and their teachers;
- identify the structure and content of this book;
- understand research underpinning approaches to the learning of children in UK schools.

A secondary school teacher explains what independent learning means to her:

> A fairly independent learner would . . . would sort of digest the task itself so the initial instructions to the task . . . and then as there are some examples in here they do tend to think about their own kind of ideas on that task. And there are some of them in here who are quite good at thinking about their own ability within that kind of task and they're fairly hooked on their strengths and weaknesses.
>
> (KS 3 teacher)

Learning is central to the classroom experience of pupils and teachers in both primary and secondary schools. On many occasions the experience for children and adults is very positive. But that is not always the case. What do we therefore already know about **learning**? I asked myself this question. That is how I came to write this book.

Between 1997 and 2001, I visited four secondary schools in the Midlands of England to investigate learning and in particular how children became 'independent learners' (Hewitt 2004). I observed many hours of lessons, and interviewed many pupils and their teachers to try to understand what we mean by effective learning. This book is my own journey towards an understanding of effective learning and how teachers can best encourage independent learning. Having set out to define effective and independent learning, I now find that my own understanding of what this means for the learner and the teacher has changed. I would like to introduce some of the ideas which have been influential in my thinking.

Defining approach of this book

Palinscar and Brown (1984) identified the active role of the learner in the development of self-regulation in classroom learning. They investigated how the strategies which learners might use to regulate their own learning could be taught. Their work has become a theoretical driving force for this research. My own experience as a teacher suggested that many learners do not always use such strategies. However, there was no specific research to inform this opinion. So rather than exploring new and innovative intervention programmes (such as those proposed by Brown and Ferrara, 1985, and Feuerstein, in Fisher, 1990), I decided to obtain evidence about the strategies pupils actually use to support and regulate their learning in the classrooms of real schools.

Sovik et al. (1994) also explained how inadequate learning strategies might be an important factor in educational underachievement. In their study of the achievement of secondary aged Norwegian pupils, they found that 18.7 per cent (grade 3) and 25 per cent (grade 8) of learners were seen to be under-performing in school. Though this research reiterated the strong link between IQ and academic performance, discrepancies between them were explained by the inability to use generic learning strategies nature (such as attention or reflection) or task-specific nature (such as the specific skills of numeracy). The differences were seen to be particularly noteworthy in boys. Though there are a number of case studies examined in this research, the concept of learning strategies is not explained in detail by Sovik et al. Categories of learning strategy such as 'task persistence' seem to be relevant, but they are ill-defined.

Not all teachers may be aware of the concept of social constructivism, but it has had a great influence on approaches to learning in primary and secondary schools at the end of the twentieth century. This is nowhere more evident than in the primary literacy and numeracy strategies implemented in English schools since 1998 (DfES 1998a).

One of the principal theorists in this tradition is Lev Vygotsky. Vygotsky was a psychologist in post-Revolutionary Russia. He died in 1934, but American and European theorists took up his ideas from the 1960s onwards. Vygotsky's ideas have been very influential for learning and teaching in schools since the 1990s.

Vygotsky explained how teachers develop 'learning potential' in the 'zone of proximal development'. The zone of optimal development is:

> the distance between the actual developmental level as determined by independent problem solving and the level of potential development as determined through problem solving under adult guidance or in collaboration with more able peers.
>
> (Vygotsky 1978: 89)

Many educational programmes in recent years have attempted to focus on the process of instruction by prescribing pedagogical structures and routines, which focus on how the teacher raises the level of skill, understanding and knowledge expected of the pupil. Developing purposeful learning, while mini-mizing boredom and the cost to the learner, are essential skills of the teacher. Critically, in this approach, learners are conscious participants in the process of learning. The pupils' interest and understanding of the learning process itself will clearly influence the learners' progress in acquiring a new skill or the ability to perform an activity. Vygotsky (1962) explains that the role of the teacher or more able peer is to model skilled performance, which the learner internalizes through a process of internal reconstruction. However, they are not always successful in achieving this.

Vygotsky (1978) famously stated that what exists on the 'inter-psychological plane' will go on to exist on the 'intra-psychological plane'. Hence external social processes go on to become the templates for internal psychological processes. Furthermore, the external control of learning ini-tially exerted by the tutor or more able peer will pass to the learner through a process in which regulation of the learning is 'handed over' by the tutor to the learner. Self-regulation by the learner is an important aim for most curricula.

Reflection

Think of a sequence of learning in which you support children towards independ-ence in a particular activity:

- What did you do to support the transition from the learners' reliance on you to their own independence in the activity?
- When they had any difficulties or misconceptions, what helped them and you to overcome them?

See Chapter 5 for further discussion.

Strategies for the classroom

Developing writing at KS2

Writing is hard! Making the links between reading and writing is very important for both readers and writers. Good readers have a better chance of developing vocabulary and awareness of the craft of the writer.

Teachers can help children develop this awareness by encouraging independent reading for pleasure and by annotating texts with children in shared reading. When children annotate the texts they read and the texts they produce as writers, this helps them to become more critical in their choice of words.

Writing conferences can be an excellent way for children to talk about their own and other people's writing. By talking to others in groups or in pairs, this can help them think through their ideas.

For younger learners, early thinking is explained as 'inner speech' (Vygotsky 1962). Inner speech is an important mechanism for directing and regulating the learning of younger children. Talk continues to be a principal mechanism by which learners regulate their own learning activity. Zivin (1979) highlights a number of theoretical models, all of which place what is called 'private speech' at the centre of the process of self-regulation. Tharp and Gallimore (1991) in their discussion of 'guided reinvention' (the process by which complex learning and problem solving occurs), highlight the fact that when under stress, even older learners revert to self-directed and self-regulating speech to manage processes and activities, which are normally automatic.

Learning is not only mediated by language, but is also essentially social in nature. This is a position that Wood (1998) considers to be agreed by many people in the field of learning. You might think that I am stating the obvious here. I am, but this has important implications for the role of the teacher and the learner.

In recent educational initiatives, there has been some debate as to the balance between the role of the individual learner and the learner as part of wider social network. For instance, the Department for Education and Skills suggests:

> Personalised learning is about tailoring education to individual need, interest and aptitude so as to ensure that every pupil achieves and reaches the highest standards possible, notwithstanding their background or circumstances, and right across the spectrum of achievement.

(DfES 2006)

Psychological theorists such as Jean Piaget would surely have supported the idea of learning in a school setting which promotes responsiveness to individuals. Others such as Vygotsky would say that the social context in which a child develops is central to the process of learning. Neither approach is wrong. An important idea in this book is that a consideration of the learner as an individual and as a member of a wider social context at the same time is entirely consistent. Learners have to adapt their thinking in response to new experiences in the home and school. Socialization involves the child developing the skills and understanding to contribute to a wider social setting, whether this is in the home or at school.

Of course, the patterns of socialization of the home may be different from those in school. This can create conflict and educational success or failure, according to the relationship between home and school. Pollard (1998: 74) questions the connotations of the learner and parent as consumer in the term 'personalization'. If the culture and patterns of socialization between home and school are different, should the responsibility for change lie with the school or 'consumer'? Or should the 'consumer' move to a school setting where the patterns of socialization are nearer to that of the home?

Structure of the book

Chapter 1 introduces some important and basic concepts and models of classroom learning. What do we mean by learning and teaching? What can teachers learn from psychologists about the promotion of independent learning? How are learning, motivation and emotions linked in the classroom?

Chapter 2 highlights some of the myths and issues surrounding learning. For instance, some initiatives have explored the idea of learning styles. Unfortunately in some cases, this has led to a superficial categorization of learners into visual, auditory and kinaesthetic styles of learning based on some very questionable assessments.

Chapter 3 provides a discussion of the various settings in which children learn. Some educationalists would argue that schools have failed to take account of the learning which goes on outside of school. Linking classroom learning in a purposeful way to the home and community can lead to more effective forms of learning.

Chapter 4 focuses on the individual learner as an active participant in the process of learning. The concept of self-support learning strategy explains how pupils support their own learning at a cognitive, social and emotional level. The concept of 'self-regulated' learning in a network of inter-dependent learners and practitioners is suggested as an alternative interpretation of what we mean by independent learning.

Chapter 5 provides a detailed analysis of the relationship between pupils' use of learning strategies and the role of the teacher. The process of developing learning strategies and support learners is discussed.

Chapter 6 considers the wider implications for schools of 'self-support learning' strategies. Examples from the primary and secondary curriculum are suggested as opportunities for developing more engaging and purposeful learning. Ultimately, this book argues that such an approach leads to longer-term improvements in learning and contributes more solid foundations to the child as a lifelong learner.

Chapter 7 concludes with a debate on the implications of self-support learning strategies for schools, teachers and pupils. The impact of so-called 'performance orientations' to learning are discussed and recommendations for a realignment of curricula are suggested. Particularly in relation to the Primary Strategy, there are great opportunities for developing the role of the learner and teacher in our schools.

The chapters are organized as follows:

- Chapter overview.
- Generic activities throughout the book allow professionals in both the primary and secondary age ranges to reflect on the professional issues suggested by various aspects of learning. This reflection process aids understanding.
- Strategies for the classroom and case studies follow each of the activities to provide the reader with a wide range of examples of strategies to support and engage in more effective learning. These draw on a range of subjects for both primary and secondary classes.
- Summary of the implications for the teacher.

I would like to take the opportunity here to recognize the importance of all adults working in school, whether on a voluntary or paid basis. Teaching assistants and teachers alike have much to gain by understanding learning. To this end, the activities which have been interspersed throughout each chapter will be as useful to teaching assistants and trainee teachers as they will be to qualified and experienced teachers. Many of the examples have been constructed so that they are accessible to professionals working with younger or older learners. Primary and secondary teachers alike will therefore find this book a useful resource.

As I was writing this book, I was thinking about all those questions that trainee and more experienced teachers ask me about learning in their class:

- Why is my class not interested in learning?
- Why does X hate what we do in class?
- Why do I have to 'spoon-feed' the children as we prepare for exams?

My view is that learning is the most important feature of the classroom whether it is in primary or secondary schools. However, teachers have a very important influence on what goes on in the classroom. With some thought and understanding of the factors which influence learning in class, a teacher is more likely to cope with these situations. However, teachers are just as much learners as pupils and I do not believe that coping is enough.

With knowledge comes understanding of challenges; with understanding comes solutions, with solutions come choices: choices for both teacher and learner. Always at the back of my mind, I have had the idea that developing confident and independent-thinking learners in school is important for schools as well as society at large.

1 Overview: What is learning?

The most valuable resource in the classroom will be found in the human form.
(Wood 1998: 227)

> This chapter will help you to understand:
>
> - theoretical and professional views of learning in the classroom;
> - models which explain learning and teaching as a complex process;
> - how motivation and cognition are inextricably linked.

Classroom context and questions

What do we know about learning in school? How do teachers see themselves? What do pupils bring to the classroom? These questions are relevant to all teachers in both primary and secondary schools. In the following extract you will find an example of one teacher's views of her pupils and how they respond to her lessons. This is a Year 9 (14-year-olds) class in a secondary school in England, but teachers of all ages will be able to relate to the views. Look at the following questions and quotes from children and teachers about learning in their school. For example, one teacher was asked why children put their hands up:

> Well, they initially wanted me to come over to see what they'd done – a lot of the groups. Others didn't know where to start at all – 'I can't think of anything' and one girl said over there 'I've just got a block.' And she must have thought of something when I read it out – the natural reaction is to think of something unless you're not listening at all. So, basically, when they were saying 'I don't know what to do' perhaps it's because I wasn't clear enough or perhaps it's because it's

Tuesday afternoon and they just can't be bothered really. Other questions that they were asking were 'Should it be in first person or third person narration?' Well, they didn't put it like that – 'Should it be I or she?' And also 'Can I have this?' And I explained to them 'You can have anything you like' but they want reassurance 'Can I have this?'

(Key Stage 3 teacher)

Can you see some of the elements of the learning process in what this teacher says? The following stages are important in any learning.

- *Knowing where to start*: 'Others didn't know where to start at all – "I can't think of anything" and one girl said over there "I've just got a block." '
- *Teacher's instructions for the task*: 'perhaps it's because I wasn't clear enough'.
- *Clarifying the learning for pupils*: ' "Should it be I or she?" And also "Can I have this?" '
- *Reassurance from the teacher*: ' "You can have anything you like" but they want reassurance.'

Pupils have their own views on how they learn. In many classes group work is seen as a very effective classroom arrangement for promoting dialogue and learning. In this Key Stage 3 class what do the teachers and learners see as their roles in learning?

We usually get ideas as a group. And then one person takes the lead. That tends to be me. Because I'm a bit more confident than other people.

(Key Stage 3 pupil)

The teacher agreed with the role of confidence in class. Learning is more than just thinking. It is more than just performing certain actions in line with the teacher's instructions. Learning is at the same time a social, emotional and cognitive process.

'Yeah. I find that across the whole school not just in this class. You always need to be giving confidence and praising them all the time saying, 'Yes that's fine', 'You can do it.'

(Key Stage 3 teacher)

How can an understanding of the social and emotional aspects of learning help both learners and teachers?

Learning and instruction

Learning is a complex concept and activity. Most teachers and pupils would recognize the importance of the social and emotional elements of learning, in addition to cognitive aspects of learning, thinking and problem solving. Many curriculum documents such as the National Curriculum for England and Wales (QCA 1999) imply a goal of independent learning. Teachers, however, often struggle to successfully develop independent learning in the classroom:

> I'm never happy with group work, as you can't pin it down. It's like, here's a worksheet, now off you go. We spend a lot of time in group work in Year 7, but what you see in the (training) videos is dream group work.
>
> (Year 9 teacher)

The teacher explains how she finds it difficult to encourage independent learning in groups. On the one hand, she wants to develop group work, but on the other she does not feel that she organizes the pupils well for effective learning. So what is independent learning? Should this be the goal for children's learning in school? Why?

In this chapter I will explain some of the common views of learning. Educationalists and class teachers talk about the need for *'independent learning' in a social context*. But what is learning? Is it a conscious or an unconscious activity? How can learning be independent when the teacher has the pressure of implementing a National Curriculum and targets driven by the need for success in tests and exams? What is the relevance of related concepts, such as learning styles, learning strategies and self-regulated learning? Some of these concepts you may have come across before or they may be new to you. They will all be relevant to professionals and learners in school.

A complex view of learning

Eraut (2000) explains that our understanding of learning should not be limited to just formal or conscious forms of learning. For instance, he considers various forms of informal learning:

- *implicit learning*, where learning is not undertaken in any conscious way, and there is no conscious knowledge of what has been learned.
- *reactive learning*, which is seen as being near spontaneous in its development. The knowledge from this type of learning is only marginally open to conscious interrogation.

- *deliberative learning*, which takes place in a planned context, and is the most open of informal learning to conscious reflection.

So much of what we focus on in the classroom relates to Eraut's description of 'deliberative learning'. Hargreaves (2005) identifies the predominance of an 'objectives model of learning' in UK schools. This involves an approach to the curriculum and teaching in which the teacher defines learning objectives in planning, which break down complex activities into a range of objectives which are 'taught' by the teacher to encourage 'learning' by the children. She explains that the National Curriculum (QCA 1999) and national testing arrangements in England have driven this. An 'objectives model of learning' and teaching tends to ignore implicit and reactive learning. Such learning is not necessarily measurable and naturally can deviate from the programme of objectives outlined in any curriculum. Hargreaves quotes Dann:

> Children are expected to demonstrate the objectives identified. They have no scope to shape, negotiate or deviate from these objectives. Together these theories underpin the role of the pupil as a mechanical agent who will react to the contexts and information given to him/her.
>
> (Dann 2002: 12–13)

Tacit knowledge is the understanding of people, situations and routines, which develops from implicit learning. Eraut (2000) points out the dilemma in investigating any forms of tacit knowledge. Though children's abilities to discuss informal learning increase the more they are asked to do this. With younger learners, the problem is compounded by their inexperience in reflection, and their limited vocabulary for discussing learning. It should not, however, be dismissed as being unimportant: as Eraut (2000: 118) says, a person may be socialized into the norms of a school or the classroom without being aware either of the learning or of what the norms of the class are. This is a very important point. Teachers and learners need to be aware of the wider view of learning. Teaching and learning operate at an explicit level in the traditional classroom activities, which we see in school, such as whole class activities to promote reading or writing in primary school, but also in the so-called 'hidden curriculum' (Pollard 1998). Teachers communicate their intentions as to the type of learning and goals of the classroom in both implicit and explicit ways.

One teacher explained that her approach to learning was 'relaxed' (in school B), and that this worked well, to foster motivation for work in class:

> I would say mine [the class] is probably the freest classroom in terms of, sort of, being able to move around and be in groups. It's also

probably the most relaxed classroom I'd have thought, I tend to be told that my classes are quite relaxed, when they're in the class they seem quite comfortable with the environment because they know the rules of the classroom and they know how it works but they also know that if they've got their own ideas they can kind of go off and do things as well . . .

I don't like a class that's very formal. I'm not terribly comfortable in a formal classroom . . . (there's) more time to be creative.

Early in September and October they were fairly boisterous . . . It took me about three months to get anything good out of them that was creative. It took me quite a long time to instil some confidence in them in their own ability.

(Year 9 teacher)

The teacher in the above classroom clearly has a particular view as to how learning most effectively takes place in her class. She emphasizes how her class is 'free' and 'relaxed'. Another teacher (in school D) said that the class atmosphere and learning were moulded by the actions of certain pupils in the class, who had adopted certain roles like 'clown' and 'leader'. The important point here is that *classroom atmosphere or ethos* goes beyond context. The classroom ethos and expectations imply judgements about learning, which have cognitive, emotional, social and indeed ethical dimensions. Pupils and teachers use various strategies to influence the affective or emotional climate of the class. These strategies may or may not improve learning or class relationships. Teachers and pupils aim to cope with the classroom situation and strategies such as taking on different roles, maintaining running jokes, or setting a certain tone in class help them to do that.

Reflection

Think about the curriculum for your class(es). How much does it build in opportunities for learners to influence the direction of the lessons, the subject matter and skills which they feel are important?

What messages do you and your classroom environment give to the learners about what you value in learning: the content, approaches to learning and class learning outcomes?

What hidden messages do you give in your choice of language and approaches to learning about the curriculum, learning and the learners?

Are learners friend or foe in your class(es)?

Strategies for the classroom

Mantle of the expert

Dorothy Heathcote is a very successful and experienced teacher trainer and educator. She developed the mantle of the expert as an essentially child-centred approach to learning where the emphasis is on a longer activity potentially spanning several days or weeks. While this is not role play, the children adopt certain roles in a scenario taking on the role of the expert. For example, a class may be asked to run an imagined hotel in their classroom. Different children adopt different roles and importantly are helped by their teacher to make their own decisions as to how to proceed. Schools that have trialled this approach explain that pupils seem to gain greatly from an academic as well as a social and emotional point of view:

1   The teacher sets a scenario and provides a purpose for the children to engage in the learning.
2   Children might be responsible for running and managing an imagined organization.
3   Critically, the children must take responsibility for the pace and direction of the activity. Dorothy Heathcote suggests that teachers' questions have a tendency to direct learning towards certain areas. They limit learning.
4   Anyone who has tried this approach will know that it requires a great deal of preparation even though children start to become more self-managing as they take charge of their learning. However, the potential benefits are enormous.

No one can possibly expect teachers, learners or classes to be perfect examples of learning. However, this question should help you to investigate your own practice, to be reflective, and to be open to constructive, engaging but challenging learning opportunities in the classroom. In the next section you will find out more about different ways of looking at learning and teaching.

Models of learning and instruction

Bruner (1986) makes the important point that cognition, problem solving and, indeed, all learning take place in a social setting, a theme very much adopted by Wood (1998). Research by Kozeki (1985) suggests that strategies for successful learning involve important motivational components of an affective, cognitive and moral nature. There is no evidence from this research that such motivational styles are fixed, but teachers, parents and peers have an important impact on these characteristics. Britton (1970) explained that the real danger when examining learning lies in imposing a separation between thought and feeling, between cognitive and affective modes of representation.

Reflection

Think of an activity or a unit of work you are or have been working on.
How have you built the following dimensions into the work?

- *Cognitive*: what skill, knowledge or activity do you want the learners to develop?
- *Affective*: what are the emotional demands of the task and how do you support this aspect of the work? For instance:
  - How do you develop a sense of purpose in the work?
  - How do you and the learners maintain motivation for activities when you confront problems in the class learning?
  - How do you and the learners judge and evaluate the learning and your teaching?
- *Social*: what are the demands of working with other people in the activity (for both children and adults)?

Case study

Primary Modern Foreign Languages Festival

Over a day, seven classes, their teachers and about 40 students led a range of activities to develop an awareness of the languages and cultures of three different countries.

Groups of students and a class teacher led each class in a morning of activities. In the build-up to this event the children were asked to find out about one of three countries.

Language activities based on Total Physical Response activities (Simon says, parachute games, etc.) helped the children to be active learners. This also combined opportunities for learners to develop social skills and empathy with people from other cultures. Some puppets from France had come to a Reception class. Their things had all got mixed up in their cases. The children had to help them sort them out so that they had everything they needed to talk about France. Not one child was dressed in a stripy shirt, onions and a beret on that day!

Bruner (1985) explains the early stages of learning a new skill or activity. The teacher or more able peer serves the learner as a vicarious form of consciousness and control, as if the teacher lends their own ability to process information or perform a skill. When the child develops control over the new skill or activity, they are then able to use the skill as a tool more widely. Critically the teacher, parent or more able peer performs the function of scaffolding the learning task to enable the child to internalize external knowledge as a tool for conscious control.

Leontev in Daniels (1993) prefers to use the term 'interiorization' to describe the process of learning, as this suggests better the process by which the child's internal psychological system is transformed actively in the process of learning and instruction. Both the learner and teacher are active participants in this process. As can be seen in the case of children's misconceptions in their developing language and conceptual frameworks, the learner sometimes constructs a wrong representation of the knowledge or activity. For example, young children in their language development frequently develop the rules for grammatical construction of words in English as follows:

Daniel: I *goed* to town to buy some Dr Who cards (past tense)
Dad: Yes we went this afternoon . . . It cost me a fortune.

Here the child makes an over-generalization in the use of the past tense in English. The adult does not correct the child but models the irregular form of the verb. In this way, children come to a way of understanding the sophisticated rules of language. Internalization of knowledge should therefore not be seen as the transfer of a package of learning from the tutor or parent to the learner. It is more like an active construction of knowledge and skills by the learner. You will no doubt recognize in your own practice as a teacher that teaching and learning can be a transmission of information from one person to another. This is not always the most effective form of teaching though.

Hargreaves (2005) talks of a continuum in views about knowledge. At one end of the spectrum, it is seen as fixed and external to the learner, and at the other end, knowledge is seen as fluid and co-constructed by the learner and teacher. For this reason many people prefer a particular approach to learning called social constructivism in which the learner is seen to be active in the construction of their own knowledge. This concept was introduced at the beginning of the book. It is now developed in the following section. While learning is seen as a social construction, the ultimate goal is regulation of learning by the learner. This is called self-regulation.

Self-regulated learning

Vygotsky illustrates the development of learning in the individual learner as a process of self-regulation. He uses the metaphor of the expert lending the novice their own consciousness, in order that the novice may be able to perform a task too difficult for them to perform on their own. According to Wood (1998), in the early years this may involve supporting important functions such as helping the learner to pay attention, concentrate or recall items from memory. Initially, early regulation enables the learner to perform tasks, but conscious understanding of the ability is only a final product of the development of self-regulation (Wertsch and Addison-Stone 1985). As the learner's ability to perform an activity increases, the need for external regulation decreases to the point that the learner can be said to regulate their own performance, hence, self-regulation. An important point to recognize here is that some pupils do not reach a conscious understanding of the activity they are involved in learning. Is this due to teaching and learning strategies which tacitly encourage superficial forms of learning? Is this due to a lack of ability in the children? These questions will be discussed at length in Chapters 4, 5 and 6.

Wood (1998) suggests that the educational success of pupils in school depends on the learner developing self-regulation in various key areas. These include the ability and desire to attend, concentrate, memorize, organize, communicate both verbally and in writing, evaluate, self-correct and self-instruct: abilities which were once supported externally.

Vermunt (1998) explains that learning is not a passive, knowledge-consuming and externally directed process, but an active, constructive and self-directed process in which the learner builds up internal knowledge representations that form a personal interpretation of his or her learning experiences. There are similarities between Vermunt's model of *constructive learning* and that of others in this field. Mental models of learning incorporate conceptions and misconceptions about the learning process. Learning orientations include the learners' views and attitudes about learning, their expectations and anxieties. Arguably passive knowledge-driven interactions, and didactic approaches to instruction are still capable of promoting learning but this is not necessarily the most effective approach.

Mental learning models and *learning orientations* influence the choice and operation of regulation strategies, which have the most direct impact on the actual processing strategies. Though it should be noted that the subjects of Vermunt's study were university students, his work does offer some interesting conceptual points. On a practical level, professionals who work with children will relate to Vermunt's conclusions: many students did not realize constructive, self-regulated, high-quality learning. Vermunt goes on to assert that the learning style of a considerable group of students can be typified as not constructive and not self-regulated, namely, undirected or reproduction directed.

An important feature of Vermunt's research is that learners mainly regulate their use of processing strategies themselves. In the context at least of university education, didactic measures (such as directions for using study skills) have little influence on the processing strategies of students. Vermunt's conclusion is that it is probably more effective to teach students to use self-regulated strategies, coupled with measures to influence the mental learning models of learners in the direction of a knowledge-constructing view. For teachers, the implications are that you can direct learners as much as you like to use certain strategies for learning, but ultimately, it is their orientation to learning and their ability to self-regulate learning that should be the focus.

Brown and Ferrara (1985), on the other hand, explained that *self-regulation* of learning is more successful in good learners and relatively unsuccessful in poor learners. The inability to exercise self-regulation of attention, for example, may be improved by teaching the appropriate strategies for self-regulation to the poor learner. They studied a number of adolescent learners, assessed as having poor literacy skills. Brown and Ferrara found that an assessment of what the learner could do with the support of an adult indicated those areas in which the learner needed help to develop their own self-regulation. This is an illustration of the movement from external regulation of the learning to internal (or self-) regulation. One important feature that the research highlighted was the children's over-dependence on adult support and (Dweck 1999) calls this 'learned helplessness':

Strategies for the classroom

Teaching Assistants and children with additional needs

It is important for Teaching Assistants not to provide too much support for children with additional needs. One particular problem is helping children to start an activity.

Having a go yourself can help the child who is emotionally resistant or poorly motivated and can provoke interest in the activity by the child This, however, should not be the same as 'doing the activity for the child'.

Supporting different parts of a task with conditional statements can help children during a task: 'I wonder what would happen if you . . .'

Edwards and Mercer (1987) were able to show that in the typical classroom, the control of the teacher was a significant factor in each of these stages. Part of the problem for pupils is that much of the process remains mysterious to them. The rather depressing conclusion they make is that for most pupils, education remains a mystery beyond their control, rather than a resource of knowledge and skill with which they can freely operate. 'In however friendly and informal a manner, they (children) are frequently asked to do things, learn things, understand things, for no apparent reason other than that it is what the teacher wants them to do' (Edwards and Mercer 1987: 158)

Government agencies would say that much has changed since 1987, however, they also go on to highlight standards of education in a significant minority of schools where the levels of learning are not sufficiently purposeful; where learners are passive and where teaching is relatively uninspiring.

In the following section, you will find out about the strategies which learners can use to regulate their own learning.

Reflection

Can you think of any occasions when adults in your class may have encouraged 'learned helplessness' in any of the learners you work with?

- What could have been done differently to encourage a more independent approach to learning?
- What strategies would you like the children to use to manage their own learning?

Learning strategies

Riding and Rayner (1998) define a learning strategy as 'a set of one or more procedures that an individual acquires to facilitate the performance on a learning task. Strategies will vary depending on the nature of the task.' This very much reflects distinctions between differences in the learner, which contribute to an individual's learning styles, and differences in the 'learning environment', which contribute to the development of learning strategies. Theoretical frameworks which explain the relationship of learning strategies to other features of the cognitive system are notoriously ambiguous and inconsistent (Riding and Rayner 1998).

Schmeck (1988) identifies some important features of learning strategies. First, they involved the conscious decision to implement a set of skills. Second, they are implemented when a situation is perceived as one which demands learning. These factors may seem rather obvious, but in examining the different use of strategies by learners in the classroom it is important to recognize that individual differences in the use of learning strategies are related to the individual's perception of their own level of control of their learning, and the impact that they can have on the 'learning environment'. These factors will be taken up in a later section, when examining the concept of perceived 'self-efficacy' (Zimmerman 1997).

Nisbet and Shucksmith (1986) suggest that learning strategies go beyond a mere string of learning skills or processes. They are almost always purposeful and goal-orientated, but not necessarily conscious or deliberate. There have been many attempts to define the nature and structure of learning strategies, often in a tentative model. For instance, Resnick and Beck (1976) made the distinction between general strategies (connected with thinking and reasoning), and mediational strategies (specific skills used to complete a task). The distinction between what is general and what is specific is not clear and the dilemma is not resolved. Butterfield and Belmont (1977) made the distinction between:

- *control processes*, which work on the information available, and
- *executive functions*, which enable the learner to sequence, evaluate, revise or abandon these operations.

The executive function appears to better capture the notion of a strategic approach to learning which is implied in the concept of a 'learning strategy'. For the teacher, the distinction offers an important focus. Since the executive functions of learning are more open to conscious reflection, they are more capable of being changed and improved through a process of reflection. These are the strategies which learners can use to regulate their own learning and can be the focus of effective 'instruction' according to the work previously referred to in Brown and Ferrara (1985).

Strategies for the classroom

Worded maths problems in KS2

Children have traditionally had some difficulty in solving worded maths problem. Modelling the different stages of problem solving using the interactive white-board can be a useful approach to this:

1 First, identify the problem and annotate the words in the problem on the interactive whiteboard.
2 Can the children remember any similar problems? What strategies did they use to solve these problems?
3 Converting the worded-problem into a more traditional mathematical calculation involves identifying the range of operations.
4 Having identified and manipulated the problem, the learner then has to complete the calculation.
5 Paired problem-solving can be especially helpful in providing learners with support through dialogue.

Having solved a worded maths problem learners should be expected to explain how to do this to each other and the class. This allows the teacher a window into the learner's thinking by making the choice of learning strategies explicit.

Reflection

Consider a recent learning activity you have been involved in (as either learner or teacher):

- What learning strategies were required to complete the activity successfully?
- How did you plan the activity?
- What strategies did you use to complete the task?
- Which of these strategies are commonly required in other contexts?
- How did you evaluate the activity?
- What demands of the learning are social?
- How do you support this aspect of the learning?

The worded maths activity described above helps to identify some of the so-called 'general' learning strategies, which might be involved in your class. Some theorists, for instance, Wood (1998) question whether there are general learning strategies. They say that many skills learned by children in class do not successfully transfer to other activities, classes or settings. Though theorists argue over a definition of learning strategies, lists of examples are strikingly similar. For example, Nisbet and Shucksmith (1986) list the following as examples of learning strategies which are said to transfer across different learning settings:

- planning;
- monitoring;
- asking questions;
- checking;
- revising;
- self-testing.

Other approaches to learning strategies attempt to establish more general frameworks. Baron (1978) identified the following:

- *Relatedness search strategies*: aimed at defining a new problem in reference to previous knowledge.
- *Stimulus analysis strategies*: aimed at analysing a task and breaking it down into its constituent parts.
- *Checking strategies*: aimed at controlling and evaluating responses to the learning task in order to arrive at an appropriate response.

Kirby (1984) similarly looked beyond concrete examples of learning strategies to a more explanatory framework:

Micro learning strategies were seen to be task specific, and more open to change, whereas macro- strategies were seen to be more generic and pervasive in nature. Macro strategies were seen to be closely related to emotional and motivational traits of the individual, but less open to direct instruction than micro strategies. Again affective factors are considered to be important in the analysis of learning strategies. It is interesting to note that Kirby's definition of macro learning strategies has similar features (generic approaches to learning highly sensitive to the affective and motivation profile of the learner) to Entwistle's concept of 'approaches or orientations to learning'.

Warr and Downing (2000) have identified three levels of learning strategies:

1   *Cognitive learning strategies*
    (a) Rehearsal: procedures to repeat to oneself the material to be learned.
    (b) Organization: procedures to identify key issues and to create mental structures, to group and interrelate them.
    (c) Elaboration: procedures to examine implications, and to make mental connections.

2   *Behavioural learning strategies*
    (a) Interpersonal help-seeking: procedures to obtain assistance from other people.
    (b) Seeking help from written material: procedures to obtain information from books, computer programs and the Internet.
    (c) Practical application: procedures which enable the learner to increase knowledge by trying things out in practice.

3   *Self-regulatory strategies*
    (a) Emotion control: procedures to ward off anxiety.
    (b) Motivation control: procedures to maintain motivation and attention.
    (c) Comprehension monitoring: procedures to monitor progress in learning, and if need be to modify learning processes where necessary.

An important conclusion made in their study of adult learners is that anxiety about the learner's own performance is likely to have much greater impact in salient, intermittent learning activities by adults than in routine, continuous school and college work. It seems that the separate application of individual strategies is less important than the balanced use of a range of strategies in a safe learning environment. Though they studied adult learners, primary and secondary teachers will recognize the 'fight or flight' response of some learners in the classroom.

Reflection

Look at the following quote about anxiety in learning: 'Failure to use a balanced range of strategies to ward off anxiety and to maintain motivation is likely to have an impact on learner performance.'

- What are the implications of this conclusion for teachers and learners of all ages when planning, teaching and assessing?
- What are the implications for teachers in terms of their own professional development and well being?

Case study

Making cartoons in a primary school

One school decided to make a film with the support of an external animation team. The cartoon depicted the seasons of the year as the children saw them through their class windows.

Every child contributed to the animation in some way: through the creation of storyboards, taking stop-frame animation clips, creating the music or by choosing the materials to be used in the animations.

Children and the teachers all got a real buzz from doing this activity over several weeks. This may not be a feasible approach to learning in every lesson, but it can have a strong motivational impact on both children and staff.

By choosing a topic of interest, which is new also to the teacher, it allows the teacher to model resilience and stamina in a longer-term sequence of learning, which for some children might be quite forbidding.

Teachers and learners need to consider the classroom environment, relationships and approaches to learning. If these do not support a constructive and positive classroom ethos, then something needs to change. Indeed, the responsibility goes beyond the teacher and learner to involve everyone in the school community, including parents.

Weinstein et al. (2000) reaffirmed the view that the learner is an active, self-determined individual who processes information in complex ways. Taking up the concept of 'planfulness' elaborated by Nisbet and Shucksmith (1986), they demonstrate how cognitive learning strategies contribute to the self-regulation of the learner. The work of Brown and Ferrara (1985) is again central in setting the foundations for the teaching of learning strategies. An emphasis on the use of learning strategies to support self-regulated learning has been shown to support an increase in the outcomes of learning (Bokaerts 2000). Weinstein et al. identified three critically important characteristics in learning strategies.

They must be *goal-directed, intentionally invoked* and *effortful*. Some research had suggested that learning strategies could develop spontaneously in the learner, but that the most effective strategies were based on models provided consciously or not in the classroom (Wade et al. 1990). Understanding about learning strategies, however, is insufficient for effective learning. The learner must know which strategy is right, how to use it and when to use it most appropriately. For example, mind-mapping may be a very effective strategy for activating prior knowledge about a topic for a writing task, however, it may be inappropriate when making choices about vocabulary in writing a piece of narrative prose (when a quicker decision might be required).

Weinstein et al. (2000) are emphatic that cognitive learning strategies do not work in isolation. Thus, just as it is important that learners know the what, how and when of using learning strategies, so it is also important to know why a strategy is important, and therefore to understand and to want to use it. Weinstein et al. describe a model of learning strategies that includes both affective and cognitive factors. At the core is the learner: a unique individual who brings to each learning situation a critical set of variables, including his or her personality, prior knowledge and school achievement history. Around this core are three broad components that focus on factors that, in interaction, can tremendously influence the degree to which students set and reach learning and achievement goals. Weinstein et al. suggested a model of learning with three components, referred to as 'skill', 'will' and 'self-regulation'.

Skill includes:

- using learning strategies;
- finding the main idea/information;
- reading and listening comprehension;
- listening and note-taking;
- preparing for and taking tests;
- using reasoning and problem-solving skills.

Will includes:

- setting, analysing and using goals;
- motivation for achievement;
- affect towards learning;
- beliefs about learning;
- volition;
- creating and maintaining a positive mind-set towards learning.

Self-regulation includes:

- time management;

- concentration;
- comprehension monitoring;
- systematic approach to learning and accomplishing academic tasks;
- coping with academic stress;
- managing motivation for learning and achievement.

Claxton (1990) suggests that learners (as well as teachers) develop '*mini-theories of learning*'. These are personal theories about the nature of learning and the school context, at a general as well as a specific level. These are formed and transformed by the context in which the learner develops. So every time a pupil enters the school, they develop and adjust their view of learning as it takes place in class and the wider view of learning across the school. Is this school focused on learning? Does this teacher value my opinions as a learner? Is learning about what I do as a learner or is it about teachers controlling what I do and what I learn?

Mini-theories develop into various forms of learning strategies:

- *Social learning strategies* might involve the pragmatic aspects of communicative competence. This involves comprehension of written and spoken language, of vocabulary and the complex structures of grammar, which enable ever more complex ideas to be conveyed. In addition to these are the range of socio-communicative strategies, such as conversational turn-taking and joking, which are so important for identity development and informal learning, especially among adolescent learners. Of course, depending on the ethos of the school and the community associated with the school, certain communicative strategies may be championed beyond others; and this is not always in line with school expectations.
- *Format of lesson files* might include ways of thinking and talking that are specific to certain subjects. As suggested in the previous section, the communicative strategies of the learner may not always be those expected to be used in school. So it should be recognized that certain subjects require different strategies. Sciences require analytical ways of thinking and learning, whereas English, for instance, requires a more personal response when reading literature. Some children rise to the challenge of the subject requirements by developing and operating the strategies successfully, whereas others do not. Unsuccessful learners often lapse into inefficient strategies such as rote learning, or indeed their inability to use the appropriate strategies may be met with rebellion and poor behaviour.
- *Intellectual learning strategies* may involve concentration, note taking and other specific study skills. Not only are effective levels of concentration and attention important for successful learning, it can be noted

that the most successful learners take an active stance to the class-room topic. This has both cognitive and social benefits. Not only will the learning process itself be optimized, but the teacher's perceptions of the learner are also likely to be more favourable. This in its own right may well ensure more positive feedback from the teacher to the learner than would otherwise have been the case. The ability to articulate confusion or misunderstandings about one's own learning is more likely to be met with positive support from the teacher or more able learner. This is the vicious circle for less able learners who are often unable to ask for help, because they are unable to recognize and articulate the nature of their lack of knowledge. Teachers could therefore draw the conclusion that the less able pupil is not interested in learning.

- *Verbatim learning strategies* include rote learning where the task requires, or the learner is unable to do more. However, there are further strategies which learners should be exposed to in school. For instance, *scripting* allows new information to be embedded in a story to aid recall. *Imagery* allows visual associations to be made between often unassociated items. *Chunking* allows groups of items with common features to be learned together. *Acronyms and mnemonics* can be used to learn lists of items, which are otherwise unconnected. *Self-testing* allows the learner or groups of learners to review information, which they might have learned by using one of the above methods, for instance, when learning spelling, or when revising for exams.

- *Practical learning strategies* involve physical skills such as the use of craft, art, science and PE equipment. New subjects can require the use of new skills, for instance, the learning of new sounds in languages. At a practical level the learner can simply imitate the activity of a more able peer or teacher. This may be ineffective if there is no understanding of why certain steps have been taken in performing an activity. Likewise if the imitated performance is not congruent with the learner's own personality or style of working, this could be an ineffective strategy for developing new skills and learning. The learner can try out new ways of working through experimentation, and practise recently acquired forms of learning. These approaches are sometimes favoured by certain teachers or curriculum areas. In any case, experimentation and practice are likely to be very important strategies throughout the curriculum. Practising itself implies repetition, consolidation and the development of automaticity.

As has been highlighted above, the choice of strategy may well depend upon the nature of the task at hand, or indeed of the expectations of the teachers and the other learners in the classroom. The development of self-regulated learning requires that pupils have the opportunity to use a range of learning strategies, and to come to an understanding of what works most effectively for them. Claxton's (1990) approach is much more focused on classroom practice than that of others based on more quasi-experimental evidence. Arguably one could categorize the learning behaviours in different ways, but Claxton's framework does present them in a way which is meaningful for classroom teachers. The framework not only relates to the successful strategies in particular curriculum subjects, but also to idiosyncrasies of particular teachers, departments, schools or regions. Pollard's (1985) and Wood's (1998) models of learning place learning in a wider social and cultural context in which teachers and learners develop strategies for coping with the classroom situation.

Claxton offers a constructivist interpretation of learning, in which children's problem-solving capacities develop from their experience of dealing with problems in real situations. Claxton suggests that play itself incorporates potential ways of enhancing learning; play-based learning in the early years, for instance, once developed for the purpose of having fun, can develop into a more generalized learning strategy for self-empowerment. The development from mini-theories to learning strategies is contingent on both successful and unsuccessful application in varying contexts. Application of the theory in differing contexts allows the activity or procedure to become more adaptable and generalizable. Unsuccessful application of the mini-theory, according to Fisher (1990), can be used by the learner to develop a tool-kit for repairing learning in future similar situations. This is a feature commonly identified in the literature of self-regulation. For example, Wood (1998) identifies strategies to repair communication breakdown, as an important high level skill.

Claxton summarizes his position as follows: 'Every learning experience is not only an invitation to improve our theories about the world; it is also an opportunity to improve our implicit theories about theory-building: to become a better learner' (1990: 101). The important point here is that the use of learning strategies develops from learning itself, and that awareness of how we learn (metacognition) also develops from learning. Learning is both reflective and reflexive.

Claxton, in line with the theoretical shift marked by Bruner, chooses to emphasize equally the social aspects of the school setting. He identifies roles that learners may adopt in certain learning situations: swot, boffin, socialite, dreamer and rebel. This is very similar to the work of Pollard (1985) in his discussion of goodies, jokers and gang members. The learning process is not always a positive experience. For instance, certain defensive strategies may be used by the learners to protect themselves from perceived problems or threats in the school setting. One example involves pupils distracting the teacher from the task at hand by more or less deviant ways.

There are two types of learning strategies: those which aid learning, and result in the development of self-regulation, and those which do not.

Case study

One teacher said:

> In my special school class, whenever I asked the children to undertake a writing activity, there was a sudden breaking of pencil leads and a long line of people at the 'pencil sharpener'. It did not take me long to realize that this was an understandable response by learners to writing activities which I had not set at an appropriate level. I could have done more to make explicit the strategies for developing independent writing skills.

Can you identify any strategies which children in your class use to avoid work?

Strategies for the classroom

Starting lessons and stepping back

Identify the main activities and skills to enable learners to make a positive start to a lesson. Make sure the children are aware of this and that you show this somewhere in the classroom if the children need to check. This could be shown visually (in pictures) or words on the board. This will help to minimize work avoidance.

Be clear about the quantity, quality and time available for any activities. This does not mean that the teacher has to wrest control of learning from pupils but it does impact on the momentum and pace of learning.

Stepping back from the class for a short time during a session will help the teacher to observe work avoidance strategies: that's if the teacher isn't already aware of them!

Claxton's analysis of learning strategies is an eclectic mix of the cognitive and affective, borrowing from psychological and sociological traditions. While a great deal of research on learning strategies has been from a psychological perspective, others have studied class-based learning from a sociological perspective. Whether one can ever talk about purely psychological or purely sociological paradigms is debatable given that cognitive psychologists often talk about social aspects of learning (Bruner 1986), and sociologists in the field of education may well identify processes of thinking that are linked to social structures and processes (Pollard 1985). However, these are two broadly recognizable traditions, and it is for this reason that both perspectives are considered. Chapter 2 will introduce Pollard's concept of 'coping strategies' to account for the strategies that learners and teachers develop to survive in the classroom.

Sociological perspectives are particularly appealing when examining classroom-learning processes, since they recognize the complexities, uncertainties and creativity of people and thus the inherent impossibility of precise verification. Pollard (1988) suggests that the sociological tradition can give a rich interpretation of the classroom, school and, indeed, the overall educational system. It is not claimed that this approach is one to be championed above that of the psychological. Indeed, the two complement each other. Even in the realms of thinking skills, there are important social elements. The following section introduces the concept of metacognition.

Metacognition

A learner's ability to reflect on their own learning is an essential component of most recent models of learning: this is called metacognition (Flavell 1976). To give a more exact definition: 'metacognition' refers to one's knowledge concerning one's own cognitive processes and products or anything related to them. It refers, among other things, to the active monitoring and consequent regulation and orchestration of these processes in relation to the cognitive objects on which they bear, usually in the service of some concrete goal or objective. Like much of the theorizing about mental processes, the concept of metacognition was seen by some as a mere 'rebranding' activity. Wellman (1981) called it a 'fuzzy' concept. However, Flavell and Wellman (1977) place metacognition in a broader framework as follows:

- *Basic operations (the memory hardware of the brain).* The most basic processes of cognition are unconscious, and are effectively the hardware of the cognitive system.
- *Knowledge component (representing the effects of attainment).* At an unconscious and automatic level, a knowledge component influences cognition.
- *Strategies,* on the other hand, are conscious behaviours, which allow the learner to 'know how to know'. These may involve strategies such as consciously rehearsing or memorizing an action prior to carrying it out.
- *Metacognition involves 'knowing about knowing'.* At the highest level, this is the knowledge a learner has of the process of learning itself: of the possibilities and constraints of the system, and of potentially effective templates for problem resolution, which have been learned from previous experience.

Nisbet and Shucksmith (1986) identify the connections between experience, cognition and goals. Following on from Flavell (1981), they describe a model of developing awareness of learning. In this model, learning strategies interact with the 'here and now' experiences of the task, the goals of the task, and knowledge about the variables of the task. These are called:

- *cognitive actions*: strategies associated with a learning activity;
- *metacognitive experiences*: awareness of learning which impacts on the task;
- *cognitive goals*: learning goals associated with the task;
- *metacognitive knowledge*: knowledge of how best to successfully complete the task.

Flavell (1981) here distinguishes between associated features of metacognition. On the one hand, the learner uses strategies (cognitive actions) to achieve certain tasks (cognitive goals). As a problem or activity is approached, the learner brings to bear their knowledge of the task, themselves and others (metacognitive knowledge) and the 'here-and-now' experience of the success or failure of the solution or activity (metacognitive experience). This is an effective distinction because it helps to explain how, as children grow older, their growing experience of problem solving helps them to deal with high-level activities and problems more effectively. Importantly, younger or less able children frequently display a *deficiency of meta-comprehension*. This is a child's understanding of their own ability in a task (what they know and when they know it). Children may be able to carry out an activity in isolation, but when asked to carry it out in the context of a task they are unable to do this (Nisbet and Shucksmith 1986).

The strategic learner of Weinstein et al. (2000) is seen as being involved in a similar sequence of activities to that suggested by Nisbet and Shucksmith (1986):

- planning to reach a goal;
- selecting methods or strategies to achieve the goal;
- implementing the methods identified in the plan;
- monitoring progress;
- modifying the plan, methods or even the original goals;
- evaluating the outcome, for the benefit of further learning.

It would seem that conscious awareness of one's own learning and thinking is a critical step in the acquisition and improvement of a learning strategies repertoire. Weinstein et al. suggest that the higher the cognitive process, the more open it is to conscious interrogation. Thus the strategic learner would be expected, according to Weinstein et al., to use the following types of information to develop learning, and to successfully carry out higher-order cognitive activities:

- knowledge about themselves as learners;
- knowledge about different types of academic tasks;
- knowledge about strategies and tactics for acquiring, integrating and applying new learning;
- knowledge about prior content;
- knowledge about which present and future contexts would be appropriate for the application of new knowledge.

Piagetian theorists devised the concept of meta-comprehension in their analysis of the link between instruction and learning. They suggest that children are ready for learning when 'they are made to know that they don't know' (Wood 1998). Cognitive conflict takes place when the teacher confronts the learner with the existence of different knowledge, and they are led to a different understanding or interpretation of the world. Though in Flavell's terms, children are often presented with opportunities to develop metacognitive experience in the classroom, without explicit teaching and modelling by the teacher, this rarely becomes metacognitive knowledge. This problem exists for learning in the home as well as in school. Several studies have indicated the inability of many parents to explain to children why their thinking was wrong, so that they may be guided towards understanding in an area of learning or in the solution to a problem (Robinson and Robinson 1982; Sibereisen and Claar 1982). Brown and Campione (1979), in a seminal paper, explained that explicit modelling and guidance by mothers lead to enhanced metacognitive knowledge and independence in learning.

Brown (1977), in a precursor to her important work of the 1980s, introduced the notion of 'production deficiency'. Young children build up a very good knowledge about learning. This is a developing level of metacognition. However, a younger learner's ability to use this knowledge in an integrated way in real learning situations often lags behind. It should be said that the purpose of activities is very important for younger learners, and like so much of the work that is carried out with younger people, it might just be that the nature of the tasks or activities that they are asked to perform lacks purpose and meaning for them as learners. As Donaldson (1978) has shown, the reformulation of a behavioural experiment, such as those carried out by Piaget, can have dramatic effects when it relates more closely to the child's view of the world. Donaldson identified the learning which some children find difficult to comprehend as 'disembedded learning'. A reformulation of a task, according to Donaldson, is sufficient to enable the child to understand the context and use a wider range of learning strategies quite successfully.

As Brown and Ferrara (1985) have stated, much self-regulation is context-bound and therefore the learners' skills do not translate between different contexts. This may be the case with many strategies, for which more mature learners have the capacity to generalize the application. Learners might be better able to regulate their learning, and be motivated in different ways for different school subjects. A child might be a surface learner in French, and motivated intrinsically by PE.

Nisbet and Shucksmith (1986) explained that as learners grow older, and their experience of learning grows and becomes more sophisticated, then the metacognitive knowledge that underpins learning strategies and the range of learning strategies will also grow. This is typical of many of the models of learning and metacognition (Claxton 1990). Lawson (1980) went further than this by saying that for normal children, increasing age is also accompanied by improved outcomes and greater accuracy of prediction about performance.

Bokaerts (2000) has developed an overarching theory of self-regulation. The work of Bokaerts and her colleagues is extremely important to an under-standing of learning in the classroom. The theory is made even more powerful by detailing examinations of classroom situations, including the use of class-room learning strategies by adolescents. To come to an understanding of self-regulation, and the use of learning strategies in the classroom, it is essential to view the bigger picture of mind, personality, and self.

Demetriou (2000) has developed an overarching theory of mind, person-ality and self. A detailed description or analysis of such a theory is beyond the scope of this review, but it is important to recognize some key features of Demetriou's model. This helps to explain the notion of self-regulation and self-theories developed by Bokaerts (2000) and Dweck (1999). In Demetriou's model the meaning-making and processing (or cognitive), the motivational and emotional (or personality), and the action (or behavioural) processes and functions, although distinct, are dynamically intertwined. Self-regulation and self-understanding develop in tandem.

Schunk and Ertmer (2000) explore the applications of Demetriou's theory in academic settings. Though much of their work focuses on the learning and self-regulation of university students, their findings are very relevant to this book. Their findings suggest that learning of content areas may not generalize to other subject areas. Self-regulation is very much content- and context-specific (Pressley et al. 1995). The suggestion is that self-regulation skills may only transfer if the learner sees the skills as being beneficial in the new context; and furthermore, the learner must possess the appropriate skills to be able to modify the processes, so that they might match the new context. Schunk and Ertmer (2000) suggest that one area of self-regulation, which might prove interesting for the future, is to examine the evidence of motivation for self-reflection in practice.

Motivation and emotions in learning

Teachers will recognize the sentiments of the following teacher:

I'd say they're quite negative. They're always ready to put their own work down and say it's no good – I don't want to read it out because it's no good. You've got the odd few – it's always the same hands going up – who always want to read theirs out.

(Teacher)

McCombs (1988) highlights the importance of motivation and emotional features of cognition, which she encapsulates in the concept of 'competence motivation'. Perceived competence is defined as a dynamic, multidimensional concept involving perceptions of one's competency in cognitive, social and physical domains (Harter 1990). Cognitive, affective and emotional features of learning are so intertwined that it is wholly appropriate to consider this wider view of learning. Harter suggests that motivation and affective reactions to perceived success or failure in learning have a causal effect on further levels of learning.

To what extent do the processes underlying the various patterns of motivation constitute learning strategies? Dweck (1999) has been at the centre of research to ascertain the role of cognition in motivation. The important point here is to identify the extent to which pupils' perceptions of their abilities and their goals affect classroom learning. There are a number of competing goals in the classroom ('having a laugh', 'getting on with male and female friends', 'gaining qualifications' and 'doing what the teacher wants you to do'). The interesting point is that despite similar circumstances and relatively similar abilities, some pupils experience positive motivation for classroom activities, and others have a more negative approach.

Dweck (1999) considers the meaning systems or beliefs about learning to be governing factors in the pupil's response to learning in the classroom. These are called 'self-theories'. The responses are heavily influenced by the way that learning outcomes and objectives of the classroom are framed. She identified two types of motivation for learning.

- *Performance orientated learning*: Some learners see intelligence as being fixed and therefore failure can be conquered only by greater effort. For these type of learners, completion of tasks is the key motivation rather than the mastery of different forms of learning. These learners are quick to denigrate their own abilities, and view their failures as fairly insurmountable under their own efforts.
- *Mastery orientated learning*: Other learners tend to see intelligence as more malleable. By changing the way an activity is carried out, their view is that progress can be made, and problems overcome. For this latter group, mastery of learning is the goal in the classroom. The learners have a positive approach to their own learning, and display emotional stamina when faced with problems.

The first group of learners are motivated by performance (task) goals and the second group by mastery (learning) goals. Licht and Dweck (1984) devised an experiment with 5th grade students in American schools to test out their theory about 'helpless' versus 'mastery-oriented' learning. Their research showed that helpless learners were more put off by initial confusions over a task compared with mastery-oriented learners of the same ability. Dweck (1999) further predicts that learners' theories about intelligence and the reasons for success in the classroom can result in depression and self-esteem loss in the classroom where their approach to learning is characterized by features of the first group above.

Bokaerts (2000) offers a link between theories of self, and the concepts of self-regulation, in learning strategies. Just as Brown and Ferrara (1985) showed that less able learners could be taught strategies to help them to regulate their own learning, so this is equally true for motivational strategies. Bokaerts reports some examples of motivational strategies:

- *Self-relaxation*: When faced with difficult situations, learners can 'downgrade' the impact of the stress, by finding meaning in past, present or future life. For instance, in the school setting a pupil's successes in school sporting activities may be sufficiently powerful to reduce the impact of the stress created by a boring and meaningless lesson.
- *Self-motivation*: Clearly one of the most powerful strategies for motivation is to focus on the positive attributes in the task itself, regardless of contingent outcomes: intrinsic motivation as opposed to extrinsic motivation.

Reinberg et al. (2000) explained that the above strategies may be insufficient for learners where the activity is perceived as being particularly negative. In these cases, a different strategy may come into play, which involves regulation of other aspects of the self-regulatory system. Control strategies can be employed by the learner in the following areas:

- *Attention control*: Active control of attention to focus on more positive features than competing negative features of the classroom situation. Working with particular books may be more motivating, when the learner can focus attention onto books that they have chosen for interest, despite the fact that literacy learning may not have the highest regard in the peer group.
- *Emotion control*: Inhibition of emotional states that might undermine the decision to attempt what might otherwise be seen as a negative activity. Reading in front of the class requires some suppression of nerves, for most learners, especially, when this is perceived as a negative activity, by the reader, and their peer group.

- *Motivation control*: The learner can strengthen the feedback for their motivational base, for instance, by regularly recognizing the small steps of progress that have been made in difficult tasks.

Reflection

Talk to one learner or a group of successful learners in one of your classes. Ask them about the things which motivate them in your classes. The above list of strategies might help you to focus your thoughts on how they maintain motivation for learning.

- Have they developed any strategies for dealing with difficult areas of learning or classroom life?
- How could you support them in maintaining motivation for your lessons?
- Look at the strategies suggested by Bokaerts and Reinberg. These might give you some ideas.

Strategies for the classroom

Learning conversations

Plenary sessions are very important points in all lessons. How do you value any lesson without some kind of evaluation at the end?

1 Avoid just revisiting the learning objectives. Try to lead the children in a discussion about how well they maintained their focus, worked independently and worked together to solve problems when they arose.
2 Learning conversations or conferences can be a useful addition. This is not about imposing targets on children. It is about providing support for them to reflect on their learning and how they maintained motivation for a task.
3 Visualization can help children see the learner they would like to be or the role they would like to adopt. Whenever learning becomes difficult, they can think about the image of who they want to become as a motivation to keep going.

If you value learning you should value the views of your pupils. What helps you to understand learners helps you to provide a better learning experience. Both learners and teachers benefit from this. In the following chapter you will gain a better understanding of the settings in which learning takes place.

Summary of implications for the teacher

Learning is at the same time a social, emotional and cognitive process

- Learning is more than just thinking. It is more than just performing certain actions in line with teachers' instructions.

The hidden curriculum contains information which can motivate or demotivate both learners and teachers

- A person may be socialized into the norms of a school or the classroom without being aware either of the learning or of what the norms of the class are.

Learning is an active process of constructing knowledge

- Internalization of knowledge should therefore not be seen as the transfer of a package of learning from the tutor or parent to the learner. It is more like an active construction of knowledge and skills by the learner.

Self-regulation is the key to successful lifelong learning

- The learning style of a considerable group of students can be typified as not constructive and not self-regulated, namely undirected or reproduction directed. It is probably more effective to teach students to use self-regulated strategies, coupled with measures to influence the mental learning models of learners in the direction of a knowledge constructing view.
- Self-regulation of learning is more or less successful in good learners and relatively unsuccessful in poor learners.

Variety and feeling safe in class learning are important for success in school

- The separate application of individual strategies is less important than the balanced use of a range of strategies in a safe learning environment. Pupils can use emotional support strategies to deal with more emotionally challenging activities.

Every time we learn something we also learn something about learning itself

- The use of learning strategies develops from learning itself, and that awareness of how we learn (metacognition) also develops from learning. Learning is both reflective and reflexive.

- Self-regulation and self-understanding develop in tandem.

Children need help to apply learning strategies learnt in isolation

- Children may be able to carry out an activity in isolation, but when asked to carry it out in the context of a task they are unable to do this.

Teachers need to help learners use their prior experience of problem solving for new problems

- As a problem or activity is approached, the learner brings to bear their knowledge of the task, themselves and others (metacognitive knowledge) and the 'here-and-now' experience of the success or failure of the solution or activity (metacognitive experience).

Know your learners' motivation for learning

- Some learners are motivated by performance (task) goals and others by mastery (learning) goals. Their views of intelligence are different and ultimately their motivation for learning is different.

2 The problem with learning

Learning? Certainly, but living primarily, and learning through and in relation to this living.

(Dewey 1900: 36)

This chapter will help you to:

- understand the differences between learning styles and learning strategies;
- question some of the myths of so called 'brain-based' learning;
- appreciate the complexities of learning in the classroom.

'Oh, yeah, we do that thinking skills thing. It's lots of worksheets. It's a waste of time.'

(Year 9 pupil)

The above quote demonstrates that curriculum developments (in this case a thinking skills programme), even with the best of intentions, do not always engage learners. In this chapter, I will explain some myths and misunderstandings about learning that are found within the educational system at present. In order to illustrate these, I will examine learning in English. This is an enormously important subject in both primary and secondary schools. There have been more government interventions and controversies in this area that in most other subjects. This will set the context for a deeper understanding of classroom learning.

Curriculum developments and learning:
English as an example

English has been the subject of great controversy during the short period of its existence, since it achieved curriculum status under the Newbolt Committee in 1921. Controversies have often centred on teaching and learning. Bennett (1989) focuses on the roles of the teacher and learner, and the extent to which aspects of English should be taught explicitly to children: the explicit teaching of grammar is one such area. English in the National Curriculum (QCA 1999) of England and Wales comprises speaking and listening, reading and writing. What role do learning strategies play in pupils' development in this subject?

The Bullock Report (DES 1975) has been hugely influential in the development and delivery of the English curriculum, and the education of 5–16-year-old children in England. When the Bullock Report was written, there was considerable concern about standards of literacy. In common with other reviews of the teaching of English (Newbolt Committee of 1921), industrial sources made the point that young people recruited straight from school frequently did not have the basic skills expected for the workforce. The report identified that as many as 2 million adults in the 1970s had not attained functional levels of literacy on leaving full-time education. This level of literacy would allow someone to read a tabloid newspaper or a recipe. Functional literacy implies that a reader or writer can operate independently in respect of the particular activity undertaken. Bruner highlights the importance of language for the development of thinking and learning in general:

> Language is a way of sorting out one's thoughts about things. Thought is a mode of organizing perception and action. But all of them, each in their way, also reflect the tools and aids available for use in carrying out action.
>
> (1985: 23)

Wood (1998) identified a change in the levels of language and literacy abilities in secondary-aged children. Whereas in the primary school (5–11 years old), the complexity of a learner's oral language is greater than their written form, this reverses at around the age of 11 to 13 years of age. Complexity here is characterized by the complexity of syntax and choice of vocabulary which allow a greater level of sophistication in the message delivered by the learner. Thus, for adolescent learners to become more independent in the use of English in its various forms, there is an assumption that this involves not only the ability to read and write a range of literary and non-literary texts. Most importantly, the learner must be able to regulate their use of a range of complex linguistic structures in both their reading and writing. Whereas the teaching of grammar was anathema to many teachers of the early 1990s, most recent programmes for the implementation of the English curriculum have been emphatic about the need to study linguistic, as well as literary structures, precisely because they allow children to develop the knowledge, skills and understanding of the very tools, which they are required to use in independent ways as they grow older.

If pupils are not encouraged to use language in order to make sense of the world, and to regulate their own experiences, thoughts and participation, then the many comments about children's lack of initiative and dependence on adult support are likely to be a continuing problem for practitioners in the classroom. Government agencies have also focused much of their work on school improvement (especially teaching and learning) in the primary and secondary curriculum. For instance, in 1997, the then Labour Opposition set up a Literacy Task Force in England to examine standards in literacy and how best this area should be achieved in the classroom. First, it defined literacy and the study of English as the development of the important skills of reading and writing, and to a lesser extent speaking and listening skills (DfEE 1998a). Underpinning this approach is the aim of encouraging the development of the various skills of English, with enthusiasm, understanding and critical awareness of the language involved (QCA 1999).

One example of an attempt to increase children's literacy skills in writing by developing their ability to implement a specified learning strategy is reported in Panagopoulou-Stamatelatou and Merrett (1996). Learners were taught to use self-management techniques for improving their writing, and for developing their own motivation for writing. Their self-management package required the children to set goals for their writing, to monitor progress towards the goals and then to select a reward for themselves if the goal was achieved. In fact, this package is not subject-specific, and could therefore be applied in other curricular areas. The results of this study showed that not only did learners produce greater amounts of writing, but that the quality of the writing improved and the children were generally more attentive. The learners in this research study were of junior school age in Greece, so it would be dangerous to infer that the same results would necessarily be replicated with older children, in England. It indicates that the use of high-level learning strategies to support self-regulation in English has an impact on efficiency in the use of the sub-skills of literacy.

The term 'independence' is not used in the National Curriculum statements of the programmes of study for English (QCA 1999). The principles of independent learning and self-regulation were never explicitly mentioned in the National Curriculum for English first developed in 1988, and revised by the various Departments for Education in 1995 and 1999. However, the higher levels indicating higher attainment in English suggest that growing independence in the use of English is indeed a requisite. The principal features of the English curriculum were encapsulated in the 'General Requirements for English: Key Stages 1–4'. For schools in England, this included the ability to communicate effectively in speech and writing in Standard English, and to become enthusiastic, responsive and knowledgeable readers. This was allied to the study of Standard English in its own right.

Since 1998, the National Literacy Strategy, and more recently the Primary National Strategy (DfES 2006), have redefined the nature and aims of literacy teaching in England. The Primary National Strategy framework now dominates the planning and delivery of English in primary schools, and since 2001 a similar Key Stage 3 strategy has been implemented in secondary schools as well. It is remarkable that the term 'independent' is part of the lingua franca of literacy teaching, now that each literacy session should include a substantial proportion of time spent in applying or practising English skills independently (DfES 1998a). Likewise it is noteworthy that though the term 'self-regulation' is now a broadly accepted concept in the discipline of psychology, it is not mentioned at all in the National Curriculum documents (QCA 1999) despite a considerable amount of work having been carried out in this area towards the end of the 1980s and the 1990s (Brown and Ferrara 1985).

A key element of learning in English is the ability to read and write a range of texts: different text-types require different word, sentence and text level choices. For the adolescent learner, the development of these skills is very much an active and conscious process, in which they need to be able to analyse different texts and recognize the function and purpose of words and sentences in a text (Wood 1998). However, with the implementation of the KS3 strategy for English from September 2001, a much greater emphasis on language study was required in the KS3 curriculum. The manipulation of texts in writing and the comprehension of texts in reading both require a sophisticated level of skills. To carry out these activities in the classroom requires the learner to be able to effectively regulate a number of sub-skills. Wood (1998) identifies the ability to manipulate grammatical structures and punctuation in reading and writing as being such important sub-skills.

A constant criticism of recent approaches to the teaching of English is that many classroom routines have over-emphasized the importance of direct, whole-class teaching methods. Burns and Myhill state that:

> More worryingly, in a heavily accountable teaching culture, highly instructional, objectives-based pedagogy seems to be required, and well-paced, teacher-directed learning is considered valuable, safe approaches. Interaction in whole class settings is, for many, currently equated with discourse patterns where pupils take part mainly in response to the teachers' questions and invitations to respond, with little extension of opportunities for use of talk to actively work on their own thinking and learning experiences. In this evidence whole

class talk is being used by the teacher for 'teaching' rather than being an instrument for learning. The emphasis on transmission of information and factual questions reflects the concern with content and the awareness of the need to meet objectives.

(2004: 47)

In a sense, hopes for independent self-regulated learning have been an illusion. The rhetoric of a so-called 'interactive approach to whole class teaching' has been a sub-conscious sleight of hand in which control of classroom discourse is wrested from pupils by the domination of discussion and questioning by teachers.

Reflection

Galton et al. (1999) in the follow-up to their research into classrooms in the 1970s suggest that learning for many children involves listening to teachers talking, whereas pupil talk was much more greatly emphasized in their original 1970s research.

- How much do you agree with this idea?
- Make a note of the balance of pupil and teacher talk in your lessons.

You might argue that there are indeed many children talking in your lesson. However, how many of them are talking about the learning? If their talk is not in support of their learning, why is this the case?

Strategies for the classroom

Talk in secondary science

In my own experience, science is often the most popular of subjects in secondary school. While it provides 'hands-on' experience for pupils, it also gives them the chance to discuss the world as it is and as it might be.

Paired talk is especially effective in helping children to predict the outcomes of an experiment.

- Ask the children to explain to each other what they expect from an experiment.
- Pupils should be encouraged to challenge predictions: 'Why does X happen?', 'How do you know about X?', 'If you did X differently, what would happen?'.

Of course none of this will happen if the teacher does not model good questioning techniques. The balance should, however, be on the pupils' use of talk for learning.

Many teachers have worked hard to focus on learning rather than teaching in their classrooms, placing responsibility for learning with the learner. One important project in this area has been the Assessment for Learning project led by a team from King's College, London.

Case study

Assessment for Learning

Black and Wiliam (1998) made a significant contribution to the discussion of learning with their study of how assessment could have a very important role in developing the quality and outcomes of school learning. Marshall and Drummond (2006) characterize assessment for learning as the 'regulation of learning', following Perrenoud (1998). This begs the question as to whether this is regulation of learning by the learner, by the teacher, or by both. Assessment for Learning is an influential concept in recent English educational initiatives, but there are many interpretations of what this means. All, however, have important implications for learning in the classroom. Hargreaves (2005) reviews the various interpretations of Assessment for Learning. She identifies six different views:

- *Monitoring pupils' performance against targets or objectives.* Frequently this relates to targets, learning objectives and improving standards relating to external examination outcomes.
- *Using assessment to inform next steps in teaching and learning.* Importantly this includes all those activities undertaken by teachers and learners, which provide feedback to modify teaching and learning.
- *Giving feedback for improvement.* This relates more specifically to the feedback given to pupils by teachers following assessment on a day-to-day basis. For instance, when marking writing, teachers might explain what went well, but what the pupil could do next time to improve their writing.
- *Teachers learning about learning.* The focus is on pupils' future learning processes rather than their future performance. Watkins (1983) makes a very important point here that 'a focus on learning can improve performance, but a focus on performance can depress performance'.
- *Children learning taking some control of their own learning.* Learners reflect on their own learning processes and how they learn in order to make improvements.
- *Turning assessment into a learning event.* This view sees pupil involvement in assessment as an integrated part of teaching and learning.

Reflection

Hargreave (2005) considers the various views of learning underpinning assessment for learning:

> Learning can be conceived as the attainment of objectives.
> Learning can also be conceived as the construction of knowledge, especially between learners and their teachers.

- What do you think about these views of learning?
- Do you find school or professional pressures pushing you towards an objectives view of learning?
- How does this impact on the outcomes of students in external tests?
- Are these views mutually exclusive?

To answer the last question, I don't think that the two positions are mutually exclusive. I do think, however, that the dominance of an 'objectives' model of learning can be very demotivating for learners, when teaching and learning lack purpose and are not seen as relevant by the pupils. Where they see the focus of learning to be purposeful and relevant, learners are much more likely to want to engage in a lesson.

Strategies for the classroom

Written feedback

The following list provides some guidance on giving effective written feedback:

- Make written feedback constructive, with some suggestions for future development.
- According to the age and development of the children, you may want to mark alongside them so that they fully understand the feedback.
- Learners should be encouraged to reply to the comments made by the teacher. In one example, the feedback conversation carried on over several days.
- The learner can ask for clarification on the feedback, make comments about how they feel about the work or say what they have done to progress their understanding.

Ultimately, this develops greater engagement with learning and assessment feedback.

Jeffrey (2003) suggested that there was little evidence of teachers incorporating learners' perspectives in teaching and learning. Bullock and Muschamp (2006) suggest that a heavily prescribed curriculum and testing contribute to a climate of dependence rather than independence and ownership, despite the rhetoric of national policy (DfES 2003). We have already seen in Chapter 1 that knowledge is constructed in a social context by learners, whereas an imposed curriculum can alienate learners. The implications for lifelong learning are important. Short-term gains of a prescriptive imposed curriculum risk longer-term alienation of learners from learning in adolescence and adult life. Few would disagree with the importance of developing the love of learning and knowledge of how to learn in a learner's early 'learning career', if they are to fulfil their roles as parents, employees and citizens later in life.

Reflection

Bullock and Muschamp (2006: 56) demonstrate that children of primary school age can be very articulate in discussing their learning:

Interviewer: What makes a good learner?

Pupil: I think they have to listen and think for themselves and think outside the question. So if you just read the question and think outside it kind of and realize what you could use from other things that you've learnt to answer and stuff.

Think about the learners you work with: how well does the above match your own experiences of learners and the learning process?

Strategies for the classroom

Pupil-teachers in KS3

While I am not advocating that pupils should be encouraged to take over the role of the teacher, some pupils can assume the role of leaders for learning. Key members of the pupil peer group will influence the way the rest of the class sees learning. This is especially the case with boys.

Convince the pupil role-models of the purpose of an activity and you will have strong advocates for learning in the classroom.

Working in small groups and listening to the pupils' views will give you the opportunity to develop a more inclusive classroom based on the interests of the learners.

'Pupil-teachers' can influence the classroom ambience and ethos: supporting a positive classroom atmosphere and expectations for learning.

The 'Assessment for Learning' movement has taken the latter conception of learning further to engage in a project called 'Learning How to Learn' (James and Pedder 2006). This builds on research dating from the 1980s on learning and metacognition. 'Learning about learning', 'thinking about thinking' and 'brain-based' approaches to learning have all been in the news in recent years as professionals try to develop more effective approaches to learning in school. Technology has provided conflicting evidence for educational programmes. It has been used to good and in other cases rather tenuous effect in recent years. Research on the brain has been used to good effect to deflate some myths associated with some 'brain-based' approaches to learning.

Brain fact and fiction

The distinction between metacognition and mere cognition is potentially problematic. A major problem relates to the potentially observable evidence of learning: some aspects of learning and thinking are neither concrete nor observable. On the one hand, thinking takes place in an observable social context, but the activities of the brain are not observable by the average professional. We can see the products of learning, but it is not so easy to observe the processes of thinking. It is true that new technologies allow scientists and medical professionals to observe the brain in operation, but we are still far from being able to link specific neurological events and specific words or concepts.

Goswami (2004) highlights some facts and myths linked to neuroscience and education. For instance, certain physical facts can be linked to learning and child development. Children with a high level of one particular gene (monoamine oxidize A) seem to be protected from developing anti-social behaviour as a result of maltreatment and poor family environments. The gene seems to limit the brain's response to stress (Caspi et al. 2002). Likewise, use of a medication called Ritalin has been shown to improve the attention of children with ADHD (Attention Deficit Hyperactivity Disorder) for visual and auditory stimulus (Seifert et al. 2003). This, however, has been seen as a controversial step by some people.

The brain is made up of two major parts commonly called the 'right brain' or 'right hemisphere' and 'left brain' or 'left hemisphere'. Though it is not controversial to say that for many people certain skills can be said to be 'localized' in certain parts or 'hemispheres' of the brain, this is not universal. For instance, language and grammatical skills in particular are said to be located in the left brain, while this is not the case for blind people or for those who learn a language later in childhood in a new linguistic community (Goswami 2004). The evidence from neuroimaging research suggests that both sides of the brain are employed in all cognitive tasks. In spoken language both right and left brain are involved in processing and producing language: left for vocabulary and right for use of intonation. Another brain myth surrounds the notion of a 'male' or 'female' brain to distinguish between so-called differences in neurological construction (Goswami 2004). Here the terms were used to talk about particular styles or approaches to learning and were not meant to represent significantly different physical entities. As Goswami says, the terms are used as 'psychological shorthand'.

Goswami explains that there are optimal periods in a child's life for certain types of learning. However, these periods are by no means 'critical' and no forms of learning are 'lost' if children do not develop at certain stages. Even the extreme cases of child maltreatment such as 'Genie' demonstrate that development can still take place later in life, be it in a much less developed way. Genie was deprived of any human contact or stimulation for a substantial part of her childhood, locked away from society, in the cruellest of circumstances. Her experience shows the resilience of children. But cognitive impairment can ensue from severe and sustained social and emotional abuse. Rutter (1975) gives the example of a girl teased about her foreign accent by her peers in school who chose not to speak at all in the classroom over a long period of time ('elective mutism'). One would think that the lack of spoken communication by this child in the classroom would severely impact on her development. That was not the case and in fact her learning and intelligence were measured as developing at normal rates.

As Nisbet and Shucksmith (1986) point out, much of the evidence about learning comes from personal introspection. Where a child is involved, the problem is further exaggerated. How can children report on what are often unconscious cognitive acts, when they do not necessarily have the appropriate capacity or language to do so? In a sense, research into learning requires detailed understanding of learning and the language associated with learning: a self-generating, self-absorbed circular process.

The skill of the teacher is to present information and activities in a way that children will understand, coaxing understanding of skills as well as the learning process itself. As children develop a consciousness of learning and language for talking about learning, so their ability to reflect on the process of learning at a more abstract and sophisticated level will develop.

Developing thinking

Nisbet and Shucksmith (1986) explained that one common approach to learning to learn, prior to the current debate on learning strategies, focused on study skills. The potential success of study skills programmes was often questioned. The development of metacognition is seen as weak when this is programmed to take place in the decontextualized approaches propounded by some study skills programmes. Where skills are taught out of context, they are unlikely to be applied in practice. Teaching the skills within the context of regular subject teaching, on the other hand, limits the capacity for transfer. The skills dilemma can only be resolved by teaching them in a meaningful context with transfer in mind. This involves bringing concepts and principles into the consciousness of the learner.

Many approaches to study skills and learning strategies have been developed as curriculum projects. The 'Self-Study Project' (Waterhouse 1983) and the Somerset Thinking Skills programme are examples. The skills dilemma resurfaces here (Kirby 1984). Broad strategies for learning are difficult to change and demand long-term application. Narrow skills, on the other hand, are easy to change or train in the short term, but are less likely to generalize. Whereas the acquisition of effective learning strategies should be the aim of any curriculum, learning to learn must be carried out in a real context, otherwise it becomes a vacuous exercise, and is likely to be demotivating for the learner. Effective teachers will set clear cognitive goals, relate activities and knowledge to previous learning and distinguish specific skills from more generalizable learning strategies. Teachers will model these processes and learners will be supported on the path towards independent control of such learning.

Though thinking skills are considered more and more in education circles (Baumfield 2006), this is rarely in the context of a wider framework of learning in the classroom. There has been a great deal of research into the use of strategies for thinking and learning in America, but this was not reflected in classroom research and practice until the late 1990s. The lack of a justification for many of the approaches has been a source of frustration for many practitioners in the last decade. Hilton (1998), for instance, sees recent experience in English teaching as being characterized by a prescription of unjustified approaches to teaching and learning. One strand of research focuses on the development of thinking skills and study skills as they relate to English. Fisher (1990) has been at the forefront of research into the development of the teaching of thinking skills in this country though his ideas have not always been incorporated into the English curriculum. His discussion of language as a subject, and language across the curriculum, gives a useful alternative perspective to that of the prescribed curriculum. This is particularly important to the review here, because it suggests strategies which children might use to improve their learning. For instance, Fisher explains how inner speech is an important tool, which children use to guide their learning and behaviour in the classroom. Children who are less successful require more support in using inner speech to regulate their learning. This corroborates the work of Brown and Ferrara (1985) in respect of the teaching of strategies to improve self-regulation in literacy. Reading is an important skill across all subjects. Fisher (1990) suggested a more general set of learning strategies for developing thinking skills in reading.

Reflection

Fisher outlined some of the questions a learner might ask in relation to a text. These questions might be indicative of the wider framework of learning strategies in respect of learning tasks:

Monitoring for meaning:	What is the text about?
Questioning the text:	Why does it say that?
Analyzing features of language:	What clues have we got?
Elaborating the text:	What will happen next?
Judging the text:	Does it make sense?
Reasoning:	What would happen if?
Reviewing:	What did you think of the book?

Of course, difference text types may provoke different questions. But how much do the learners in your class(es) ask these questions when they read a text. Who asks the questions in your class(es)?

As one of my colleagues said on entering a career in Initial Teacher Education: 'After a year, I've realized it's not about me (the tutor) it's about them (the learners).' My colleague was noting the importance of a focus on learning and the learner rather than teaching and the teacher. The following example shows one way of involving children actively in their learning.

Strategies for the classroom

Going on a Bear Hunt (Rosen and Oxenburg 1993)

This book can be used in so many different ways:

- Go on a bear hunt with the children, singing the words in a chant echoed by the children.
- Older children could make up their own version of the picture book, younger children could act out their own hunt (a 'treasure hunt', etc.).
- Readers could be asked to look at the use of colour and direction in the book.
- Which parts of the book are in black and white or in colour and why?
- Look at the direction the children are walking. How does the section at the end of the book help younger readers to recall the events of the story?

A number of educationalists have applied Vygotsky's ideas in developing programmes for self-regulation in pupils with learning difficulties. One of these researchers is Feuerstein. Brown and Ferrara (1985) reported Feuerstein's research which showed that there is a subset of low achieving learners for whom a small amount of help in the development of regulatory functions will result in a significantly large increase in their ability to perform tasks. Feuerstein calls this set of learners true underachievers since they are not strictly cognitively impaired. Feuerstein developed a framework called 'Instrumental Enrichment' (Fisher 1990). This used an abstract set of activities, which involved developing children's use of thinking and learning strategies. The role of the tutor is to support the learner in coming to a greater understanding of the thinking and learning strategies which they use to solve the problems presented to them as part of the 'Instrumental Enrichment' activities. Fisher (1990) reports some very significant gains in traditional intelligence tests for learners with special needs in particular. Many teachers will recognize the importance of dialogue in developing children's understanding. For instance, in the teaching of primary maths, it is seen as being very important to ask children to explain the strategy they use to solve problems. By explaining the methods they used, this helps other pupils in class to understand the steps involved in successful problem solving. A pupil's explanation of the approach to a problem will also expose any misconceptions or other problems of understanding.

Runco and Chand (1994) review different types of problem solving: presented and discovered problems. On the one hand, the features of the problem are set out for the learner (for example, in the case of the traditional maths problems in which the learner has to calculate a numerical answer from given variables). On the other, the learner has to identify those features for themselves. In the latter case, the learner is involved in both problem finding as well as problem solving. As Einstein is reported to have said (Einstein and Infeld 1938), the formulation of a problem is more essential than its solution. Runco and Chand (1994) identify a learner's ability to find and solve problems as being significantly predictive of creative abilities. However, the limited experience of younger children in both problem finding and problem solving often engenders more creative approaches to the problem, in order to overcome a lack of experience.

Donaldson (1978) showed that some pupils fail in schools because they have not mastered the disembedded forms of thinking which are currently valued in western education. If we think that low ability pupils have not experienced the strategies which more able pupils experience in more supportive home settings, do we then risk alienation of lower ability pupils by compensatory forms of education in which problem-solving strategies and stances towards learning run counter to those espoused by parents and the social background of the pupil? Before such questions can be answered, the nature of learning and instruction must be explained, as the notions of what it is to learn and teach are important foundations for the theoretical discussion of learning strategies.

There has been significant interest in recent years in how children learn.

This has not always been underpinned by evidence of learning and research. One particular area of confusion has been 'learning styles'.

Learning styles and strategies

The term 'learning styles' refers to qualitative differences among individual students' habits, preferences or orientation towards learning and studying (Sternberg 1997). One interpretation of learning styles relates to the mode in which learners supposedly process information most effectively. This viewpoint is expressed by the following:

> Each of us has a natural preference for the way in which we prefer to receive, process and impart information. This is largely genetically determined but is also susceptible to development, particularly when we are young (while our neural pathways are still being established). There are various ways in which preferred processing modes become apparent and some simple ways in which we can enhance the effectiveness of our communication once we are aware of them. One way to detect a person's preferred processing mode is to watch their eye movements, particularly when they are thinking or answering a question.

Visual thinkers will tend to use and respond to terms such as:

- I get the picture.
- I see that now.
- From my perspective.
- What's your view?

Auditory thinkers will tend to use and respond to terms such as:

- I get the message.
- That rings a bell.
- That strikes a chord.
- Sounds OK to me.

Kinaesthetic thinkers will tend to use and respond to terms such as:

- How does that grab you?
- A grasp of the basics.
- It certainly feels right.
- I can relate to that.

(www.brainboxx.co.uk)

Despite the fact that this web-site uses the term 'thinkers', it implies that learners have particular preferences for the ways they learn and process information (learning styles). Such approaches tend to suggest ways of assessing learners' preferred leaning styles. It is then suggested that activities which complement the preferred learning styles should be included in the activities set up by teachers to support learning.

The overwhelming popularity of modality theories of learning styles contrasts sharply with the unsupportive results of research on these models (Kavale and Forness 1987; Snider 1992; Stahl and Kuhn 1995; Yates 2000).

Klein (2003) says that the emphasis on differences between individuals' cognitive abilities, and the assumption that curricular tasks correspond to such differences in a one-to-one fashion, are theoretically incoherent and empirically mistaken. He argues that:

- Most educational tasks employ multiple, complementary sign systems.
- Most educational tasks engage many cognitive resources;
- Interactions between cognitive resources and curricular representations are dynamic, complex and task-specific.

(2003: 46)

Howard Gardner (1999) suggests that humans have seven intelligences, to which he later added an eighth. Gardner went beyond many theorists by recognizing a very broad range of abilities as cognitive. He suggested that each of these abilities was an intelligence, rather than as a component of one global intelligence. Gardner describes intelligence as: 'a biopsychological potential to process information that can be activated in a cultural setting to solve problems or create products that are of value in a culture' (1999: 33–4).

Each of the eight intelligences of Gardner's theory addresses a specific domain:

- linguistic;
- logical-mathematical;
- spatial;
- musical;
- bodily-kinesthetic;
- interpersonal;
- intrapersonal;
- natural.

Each person possesses all of these intelligences, but they typically differ in the strength of each intelligence.

Case study

Consider the following fairly typical primary classroom activity. Children have been asked by their teacher to read a range of books about the Egyptians to extract some information about pyramids. What modes of processing might be involved in this task?

The following might help you recognize the complexity of tasks.

- In reading, it could be argued that there is visual processing of words and pictures; sounding out of words involves the phonological (auditory system); while turning the page or following the text involves physical (kinaesthetic) activities.
- What about writing, discussion in pairs or examination of artefacts?

Strategies for the classroom

Investigating your home town using Internet Census resources

The Internet provides very accessible resources for investigating the historical aspects of your locality. Internet texts often require different ways of reading and investigation: using search facilities, identifying key words, navigating radial as opposed to linear texts:

- Pupils could read entries in the sites to find out about the lives of people: their jobs, family structures, changes in families over time.
- Comparison with the locality now and in former times provides the opportunity to express facts in different ways.
- Mathematical facts can be expressed in different ways: graphs, tables and diagrams.
- Historical events can be expressed from different points of view: in writing and dramatically in role.

I agree with Klein (2003) in his critique of the overly simplistic view of learning styles and intelligences, which has been explained above. I do, however, believe that the discussion provoked by proponents of the 'science of learning styles' has made an important contribution to education because it has encouraged professionals to question the processes underpinning learning and pedagogy. Some of the INSET and published materials in this area fail to provide sufficient evidence to justify claims about particular approaches to 'learning styles'. Some research takes a less simplistic view of 'learning styles'. This has had less prominence in educational circles. For this reason, I will review some of the evidence below.

Riding and Rayner (1998) identify a considerable evidence base for a con-nection between learning strategies and learning styles. They outline a very interesting account of how learners modify features of the learning situation, so that they are more attuned to their own learning styles. For instance, an 'Imager' may 'translate' a text of words into a diagram, an 'Analytic-Imager' may not be able to obtain an overall perspective of a problem as a 'Wholist' might, but they may be able to adapt to the constraints of the activity by generating an image of the whole. Reduction of high processing loads in one mode of learning can result from the redeployment of attention from one form of information to another. For instance, the processing of large chunks of text may be difficult for an 'Imager', but may be facilitated by selective scanning of the most important sections in order to save reading the whole.

Riding and Rayner's own examination seeks to distinguish between learn-ing strategies and learning activities. Learning is seen as being strategic when it is particularly appropriate for the learner. This is a rather weak, subjective and circular definition of learning strategies. To say that learning is a strategy because it is strategic is unhelpful. A strategy implies a decisive and considered approach to the positive solution to a learning task or activity. To what extent the development and operation of the learning strategy are open to conscious reflection, operation and change, is debatable. However, such a definition would seem to be more powerful.

Kozeki (1985) suggests that certain *motivational styles* result from the reinforcement given by parents, teachers or peers. They are marked by domin-ance of affective, cognitive or moral motives in learning. Accordingly, Kozeki's study of the motives of successful school learners, for instance, noted that learners who scored high in the cognitive domain, but for which the moral domain of motives was dominant, were concerned with self-improvement, fulfilling expectations and playing according to the rules.

Riding et al. (1995) are typical of many theorists in the field of cognition in distinguishing between various levels of cognitive process. Riding and his colleagues are at the forefront in their description of this distinction. Cogni-tive style is defined, by Riding et al. (1995), as an individual's characteristic and consistent approach to organizing and processing information. It is considered to be a fairly fixed characteristic of an individual, whereas cognitive strategies, the ways that may be used to cope with situations and tasks, may be learned and developed. Various researchers have investigated the nature of cognitive style (Riding and Buckle 1990). Riding et al. (1995) identified two basic dimen-sions of cognitive style: Wholist-Analytic, and Verbal-Imagery styles. In a later paper, Riding and Rayner refined their definition of what they went on to call *learning styles:*

> an individual set of differences that include not only a stated personal preference for instruction or an association with a particular form of

learning activity, but also individual differences found in intellectual and personal psychology.

(1998: 51)

Entwistle (1985) identified the impact of the learner's intention on their orientation or approach to learning. This very much focused on the different levels of cognitive processing. Learners were seen to process information in a 'surface or deep' manner. Surface learners, subject to extrinsic motivation, tend to focus on the structural aspects of a task, whereas deep learners, motivated by the intrinsic factors, tend to focus on meaning. Entwistle showed that there is a correlation between learners' motivational styles and their approach to learning. For instance, deep learners are motivated by the intrinsic features of a learning activity, while surface learners are motivated by the fear of failure. There is a problem with such categorizations. Remember that learners can perform differently according to the task and subject area, so it may be dangerous to label children as one type of learner rather than another.

Strategies for the classroom

Museums and art galleries as classrooms

While technically not in school, these spaces provide great possibilities for purposeful learning in authentic settings:

- The wide expanse of a landscape can capture the imagination of a child to explore the character and settings in the story of a painting.
- An industrial museum provides a sense of scale for machines which in books can seem bland and uneventful. Face-to-face, a working steam engine comes alive.
- A local museum especially can develop a child's sense of place. Seeing photos of children in your school from 50 years ago does develop a deeper understanding of the history of the school and local community.

Beware, though, of superficial engagement with out-of-school learning. Running around a museum at breakneck speed, pushing and pulling as many knobs as possible does not necessarily develop a good understanding of the exhibits.

A more structured and active engagement followed by activities back at school to further develop understanding is more likely to lead to less superficial learning. Digital photos from a school visit can personalize the follow-up activities more for pupils.

Reflection

It can be helpful to analyse different levels of performance as giving evidence of potential approaches to learning.

- Do you recognize any learners in your class(es) as either 'deep' or 'surface' learners?
- How do these learners vary in their motivation for learning?

It is not within the scope of this review to explore in detail the concept of cognitive style. However, it is worth noting, based on the research of Riding et al. (1995), that 'Imagers' learn best from pictorial presentations and 'Verbalisers' learn best from verbal presentations. Furthermore, in earlier research (Riding and Dyer 1980) personality attributes were found to be correlated with the aforementioned cognitive styles. For instance, 'Verbalisers' were seen to be extraverts, outgoing and lively, whereas 'Imagers' were seen to be introverts, polite and restrained. These points are important in supporting the view that social, emotional and personality attributes are all important factors to be examined in the study of children's learning.

Schmeck (1988) differentiates between *learning tactics* and learning strategies. In his model, tactics refer to the specific activities of the learner: they operationalize tactics, in specific situations. Learning strategies, on the other hand, are considered to be more general, operating at a higher level. In fact, a learning strategy dictates the use of a cluster of tactics in the achievement of a specified learning outcome. For McCombs (1988), and Riding and Rayner (1998) affective factors are seen as underpinning the cognitive system. Through different theoretical positions they identify different forms of learning styles. These are seen as influencing the development and operation of learning strategies. Note Riding and Rayner's (1998) explanation of how the use of adaptive learning strategies can help overcome the limitations of certain learning styles. Strategies to overcome the limitations of certain learning styles work at the affective and social, as well as the cognitive, level.

'Affective' and 'effective' learning

McNess, Broadfoot and Osborn (2003) investigated teachers' concerns over the conflict created by growing workloads and the 'tension between the requirements of government and the needs of their pupils'. They highlight the impact of government policies focused on teacher and learner performance of what is centrally measured or analysed as 'effective'. The 'effective' learner and teacher are contrasted with many primary school teachers' beliefs about the importance of the 'affective' aspects of teaching and learning. Clearly, it would be utopian to suggest that teachers or learners should fall outside the boundaries of accountability; however, McNess et al. suggest that an over-emphasis on the so-called 'effective' can damage the quality of learning. Much learning is not measured in formal tests in school and later in life. The danger is that an over-emphasis on the 'effective' can result in less effective learners in the wider and long-term sense.

Dweck (1999) in her explanation of the link between self, motivation and cognition explains that people develop beliefs that organize their world and give meaning to their experiences. Dweck suggests that different people create different 'meaning systems'. People create meaning systems in order to explain their own learning, their interactions with others, their understanding of the reasons for success and failure, and most importantly their understanding about themselves. Beliefs about the self (called 'self-theories' by Dweck) have a tremendous impact on the psychological, affective and cognitive realities of individuals in similar situations. Dweck's work is very powerful in explaining how different learners under similar circumstances respond in different ways, with varying outcomes and motivation patterns. Like many other theorists from the socio-cognitive perspective, Dweck sees the learner as an active constructor of their own understanding. Like Claxton (1990), Dweck focuses on the learner's development of theories about learning. Such theories can lead to learners seeing themselves as helpless and negative subjects of fate, unable to change the way they learn, in order to make progress. Dweck sees intelligence, motivation and self-image as being malleable and interconnected features of the learner. This approach is adopted by Bokaerts (2000) in his model and explanation of self-regulation, which will be explained in more detail later.

In the same vein as Dweck, Zimmerman and Martinez-Pons (1990) explain how learners' perceptions of academic ability (perceived self-efficacy) can impact on achievement. Theories of self-regulated learners view students as metacognitively, motivationally or behaviourally active promoters of their academic achievement. Zimmerman and Martinez-Pons see learning strategies as enabling students to regulate their behaviour and environment as well as their covert functioning. Most importantly in the work of Zimmerman, the learner's perceptions of academic *efficacy* (effectiveness) are seen to have a direct impact on motivation and future perceptions about their ability to realize potential academic ability. Where learners are aware of deficiencies in their performance, this will reduce future levels of self-efficacy. If you feel bad about your performance now, it is likely that you will feel even less positive the next time you undertake a skill which you previously found too difficult. The group of American students, from a diverse ethnic background, and with control groups for average and gifted learners, demonstrated that the more able the learner, the more likely they were to use a wide range of learning strategies.

Furthermore, the older the pupils, the more likely they were to use learning strategies successfully.

As one of my colleagues once said in respect of learning: 'The rich get richer and the poor get poorer!'

Summary of implications for the teacher

Talk is important for developing thinking and learning in general

- If pupils are not encouraged to use language in order to make sense of the world, and to regulate their own experiences, thoughts and participation, then children's lack of initiative and dependence on adult support are likely to be a continuing problem for practitioners in the classroom.
- Inner speech is an important tool, which children use to guide their learning and behaviour in the classroom.
- Encourage children to explain the methods they used in solving a problem.

Self-management strategies can improve writing and other areas of the curriculum

- Self-management requires children to set goals for their writing, to monitor progress towards the goals and then to select a reward for themselves if the goal is achieved.

Whole-class teaching is not always the most effective for developing interactive learning

- 'Pacey' whole-class teaching dominated by teacher questioning is not necessarily interactive and effective in developing understanding beyond superficial levels.

Turn assessment into a learning event

- Assessment for learning should enable children to take charge of their own learning, whereby assessment is an integral part of learning and teaching.

Beware brain myths

- Both sides of the brain are employed in all cognitive tasks. In spoken language both right and left brain are involved in processing and producing language: left for vocabulary and right for use of intonation. But this may be different for visually disabled and left-handed children.

- No forms of learning are 'lost' if children do not develop at certain stages.

Don't jump to simplistic conclusions about the 'learning styles' of your pupils

- Learners can modify features of the learning situation, so that they are more attuned to their own learning styles.
- An 'Imager' may 'translate' a text of words into a diagram, an 'Analytic-Imager' may not be able to obtain an overall perspective of a problem as a 'Wholist' might, but they may be able to adapt to the constraints of the activity by generating an image of the whole.

Teach skills in context, but encourage pupils to apply them in other situations

- Effective teachers will set clear cognitive goals, relate activities and knowledge to previous learning and distinguish specific skills from more generalizable learning strategies.
- Teachers will model these processes and learners will be supported on the path towards independent control of such learning.

Short-term gains in standards can be at the expense of longer lifelong learning

- Much learning is not measured in formal tests in school and later in life. The danger is that an over-emphasis on the 'effective' can result in less effective learners in the wider and long-term sense.

Develop positive views of learners' own views of their ability

- Encourage, a can-do approach in which the learner takes control of their own learning with limited support from the teacher.
- Intelligence, motivation and self-image are malleable and interconnected features of the learner.

3 The competing social settings of learning

If teachers close their eyes to learning which occurs outside of school, and are required to impose school models of learning onto children's home learning, they miss important parts of the whole picture of learning.

(Maddock 2006: 154–5)

This chapter will help you to:

- learn about the importance of self and context for learning;
- develop an awareness of the impact of the school setting on children's learning;
- understand how teachers and learners develop coping strategies to deal with the classroom situation.

Many people involved in education promote the importance of independence and meaningful learning experiences. The home, school and peer culture often provide competing demands and attractions for a learner. Different contexts provide different opportunities for learning. These will be explained, especially in relation to the children's own views about their learning. The 'context for learning' is an important concept which will be developed further in this book. Learning was reviewed in detail in the last chapter. But where does this happen? Do we just focus on schools or should we consider learning outside of school?

The wider context for learning

Bullock and Muschamp (2006) report their research into the views of 24 Year 6 pupils. There was a mixed view as to whether schools genuinely responded to their views and built in their perspectives. Recent government policies such as

Excellence and Enjoyment in primary schools, for example (DfES 2003) demonstrate overt commitment on the part of the authorities to 'personalised, more individual approaches to learning'.

Maddock (2006) reviewed a range of studies of children's experience outside of school. For example, Brice-Heath (1983) and Tizard and Hughes (1991) showed how pupils used language and literacy practices in different ways in the home environment compared to that of the school. Role models, cultural artefacts, experiences, tools, time, spaces and places all provide a context through which learning develops. A failure to recognize the home culture could lead to a mismatch between school and home. Important values of the home and school community may not be mutually reinforced: fertile grounds for underachievement in school.

Maddock (2006: 156) views the child from three perspectives:

- the child the teacher knows;
- the child the parents know;
- the 'third child', an unknown child, the person the child was becoming and wanted to be.

She explored the experience of 8-, 9-, and 10-year-old school children in England. All children were judged by their teachers to be unlikely to achieve the National Curriculum benchmark levels by the end of primary school. Children talked about their experiences of riding bikes, playing football, playing computer games and taking part in family activities like boating:

> Although the children were engaged in the same activities which, on the surface, involved them in similar learning, at a deeper level their learning was very different. The activities served different learning purposes for each child, and children used them to make different connections between the activities and their unique personal lives. Consequently, whereas at first children were seen learning the same things in different contexts, now, conversely, children could be seen engaged in different learning in the same contexts . . . most of the children played football. This involved them all in learning the rules of the game, how to kick and control a ball, work as a team member, balance and score goals for example. However, again, the personal learning was diverse and ranged from learning about professionalism, success and failure; through tenacity, having a go, fitting in with friends and mastery; to being a tomboy and being socially acceptable.
>
> (Maddock 2006: 160)

Maddock paints a very rich picture of children who manipulate contexts out of school to meet their own learning interests. Children would play out their anxieties or desires according to their current concerns. 'Transformation' is the term coined by Maddock to describe the way children appropriate opportunities to suit their own ends. Interestingly, children could transform ultimately different contexts to arrive at the same deep learning.

Reflection

What do you know about the children in your class(es)? Remember that learning goes on inside and outside of school. They might have different attitudes to learning outside school. They may not even consider this as learning.

- What are their experiences outside of school?
- Does the school learning connect with the learners' experiences outside of school?

Strategies for the classroom

Building on prior learning in secondary schools

Most teachers agree that learning should always build on prior learning. There can be a tendency to only consider school learning. But there are ways to be more inclusive of all forms of learning:

- Concept maps are a good way for teachers and pupils to understand what they already know about a topic: in and outside of school.
- Working in pairs, learners can find out about their partner knowledge or any relevant experience.
- Teachers need to share their own lives out of school with their class. While some teachers may feel uncomfortable with this, it helps the children to see the teacher as a more human figure, to develop trust and therefore to be more willing to share their own experiences.

Holidays, part-time jobs, caring for relatives and siblings, local building developments, significant local events like accidents and crime all provide the backdrop for learning, developing coping and problem-solving strategies, all of which may be relevant to a new area of school work.

Maddock reinforces the views of many other commentators in the previous chapter. Learning is more than the successful performance against predetermined learning objectives set within national frameworks. Teachers must be aware of the transformative nature of learning. Furthermore, learning should recognize the value of children's experiences outside of school.

The notion of informal learning outside the formal setting of school is an important area:

> 'Situated learning' and 'situated cognition' challenge the traditional approaches of education and psychology. Instead of regarding learning and cognition as universal processes and studying learning as a decontextualized one, there is now an interest in viewing learning as situated and bound to specific settings.
>
> (Andersson and Andersson 2005: 421)

Andersson and Andersson explain that cognitive processes do not develop in a 'cultural, historical and institutional vacuum'. They compare the learning of adult Somali refugees in Sweden. On the one hand, they learn in a more traditional formal educational setting. They also learned about Swedish society in so-called 'non-formal' education. In this approach, members of the Somalian community and the learners themselves were involved in planning and implementing the courses. Outside speakers were invited to the group to speak about issues of immediate interest to the group. Andersson and Andersson found that learners took much greater responsibility for their learning in such settings.

Case study

At the start of their experience of learning in Sweden, one of the Somali participants said:

> I do not trust the system. I do not think that the system is for me. I am an outsider. I came to a functioning system, which I do not understand and therefore I cannot make up my mind, I pull back and I have problems participating.
>
> (Andersson and Andersson 2005: 427)

You could say that these are adults. These are refugees in a country far from their homeland. This is Sweden. They are not learning about subjects in a school curriculum.

But consider learners you have taught. Would any of them have said the same as the Somalian refugees in Sweden? If they might have, then we ought to consider the various settings for learning in more detail. There may be something in this for all of us!

Strategies for the classroom

The extended school project

It is possible to differentiate activities and learning by 'interest'. In this approach to planning and learning, pupils have a degree of responsibility in planning and choosing the topic and content of their work within broader parameters. Not all activities can be studied in this way, but if used judiciously throughout the year this allows learners to choose areas in which they are interested.

Children need help to sustain their interest and to scaffold the process of planning an activity, researching a project and presenting some kind of report at the end of their project.

A shared understanding of project outcomes should not be confused with strict guidelines which impinge on the structure of the project. The beauty of this approach is that it provides learners with the duty to take responsibility and produce something a little more original than filling up boxes on a multiple choice.

Andersson and Andersson (2005: 423) explain their notion of 'authentic pedagogy' as a way of understanding the physical and social contexts of learning. Put simply, 'authentic learning' involves 'activities which are personally meaningful to the learner – that is engaging and relevant in a way that assists them in their own meaning making'. For mainstream learning provision, there is a great deal to be learned from this approach. They do, however, counter the potential view that schools are in some way deficient. On one level, the school setting is an authentic one for pupils in that schools help children develop skills and knowledge to succeed in school. On another level, schools should try to understand the learners' perspectives and interests for certain topics which are situated in real activities in real situations. There are links to the concept of 'lifelong learning', where adult learning is situated in everyday activities. This is a very important point.

Should we consider mainstream school learning as a preparation for life-long learning? Or is mainstream school learning part of the lifelong learning process? If we agree with the latter view, then children's learning in primary and secondary schools is merely one, be it very important, part of the continuum of 'lifelong learning'. The principles and contexts of lifelong learning, as suggested by Andersson and Andersson, then provide important support for a review of the contexts and settings of primary and secondary schools.

The school setting

In my investigation of self-support learning strategies in Year 9 English classes, teachers and pupils had different perspectives in respect of teaching in the school context. One such area was that of the curriculum. For example, whereas teachers tended to emphasize the curriculum objectives of literacy, and the importance of these skills for both reading and writing, the pupils had a very different view. Pupils in one school saw literacy as a lesson in which they did worksheets, relatively decontextualized from the other aspects of the curriculum. The pupils were not very favourable in their comments. One teacher recognized this as a problem throughout the school:

> It does them good to have a lesson where they're looking at an extract and saying 'Why is that effective?', 'Why is that good?' But I certainly don't see the point in taking it apart, and taking it apart just so they know mechanically really, how it's put together. I mean, the thing about writing is its enjoyment – you're supposed to enjoy it – it's an art and I think that English teachers tend to forget that at the end of the day, with the mechanics.
>
> (Year 9 teacher)

On the other hand, pupils saw these lessons as just another 'bunch of boring worksheets'. They said that they were not very interested in this approach or this topic.

Pupils often had a different and unexpected perspective on the use of school resources. For instance, though every Year had at least one lunch-time library session a week set aside for their sole use in one school, the pupils said that they often tried to sneak into the school library at lunchtime, in order to escape the cold and bad weather!

Gender was an important feature of the social dimension of the classroom. A feature of the attitudes to learning of both boys and girls was a perceived lack of confidence in ability: even where pupils were judged to have ability in English, their own perceptions were lower. This was particularly marked for boys. For instance, a teacher in school B said:

> I think, particularly some of the boys in here, (are) very negative when they came in, very under-confident some of them, and I think that over the year overall, they've done, over the last few weeks they've done well.
>
> (Year 9 teacher)

This same teacher went on to discuss some of the different approaches to learning between boys and girls in her class:

> The boys sit in much more mixed ability groupings, whereas girls tend to sit with people of the same sort of ability – even though they are in friendship groups, do tend to be with people who are as able as them.
>
> (Year 9 teacher)

Her views that boys tended to prefer to sit in larger groups and girls in smaller groups or pairs were borne out in observations of other classes in the research where pupils were allowed to choose the places where they sat. According to teachers and pupils, girls tend to choose friends of similar academic abilities, whereas boys tend to choose friends of differing academic abilities. Therefore when given a choice of who they can sit and work with (groupings were predominantly based on friendship), girls would sit with like ability, and boys with differing abilities. Furthermore, it was suggested that girls prefer to work in smaller groups (pairs or threes), whereas boys prefer to work in larger groups (fours or above). One very large group of ten boys worked quite effectively, but for planning purposes, they worked in smaller sub-groups of about three, where a smaller forum was better. Given the choice to work in mixed or single-sex classes, most pupils would choose to work in mixed-sex classes; not, however, for academic reasons, but because the pupils 'have more of a laugh'. In fact, there was some debate as to whether single-sex lessons favour girls, but not boys, whereas mixed-sex classes favour neither, at an academic level. Boys tend to be more gregarious in their work. Humour, sarcasm and imitation are all strategies for use in the lesson. In one lesson mock fighting of a particularly brutal nature was observed, which boys dismissed as 'two friends having a bit of fun'. Boys consider these strategies as very important ways of allowing them to cope with the perceived tedium of some lessons, and with a subject which some of them consider to be 'uncool' (Hewitt 2004).

The teacher invariably sets the goals of any lesson; however, pupils often have choices as to how they will reach those goals. Affective goals, however, are invariably set by the pupils. This could be in terms of popularity with peers, which will result in greater motivation for engaging with a task or performance in the longer term. Though exam success was seen as an important goal by teachers, pupils had more personal long-term goals. One pupil in school C said that she wanted to do better than her sister in the GCSE exams (the grade itself was of less importance).

Two theorists in the field of sociology have examined the problems, issues and contradictions associated with teaching and learning in the classroom: Hargreaves (1984) and Pollard (1985). The learning they examine takes place in real classrooms. This potent feature is extremely appealing to practitioners, and those involved in the development of classroom procedures. As Pollard

(1988) reports, principles are believed to be true when they give rise to actions that work. Such knowledge does not have to be open to elaborate expression. It simply has to 'do the job'. However, what practitioners and indeed pupils mean by 'doing the job' is very much open to discussion.

As Hargreaves (1984) states, education and society cannot be studied in isolated realms. Hargreaves is not the first to confront the seemingly endless list of contradictory issues, dilemmas and challenges, which are played out in the twenty-first-century English education system. On the one hand, there is a democratic liberalist tradition of pluralism and inclusion. On the other, a strongly polarized system results in many children of middle-class families being educated in popular well-resourced schools which are effectively closed to working-class pupils because of where they live. Teachers and parents espouse creativity and independence in learning, while a draconian central-ized government department oversees a highly prescriptive curriculum. Pro-gress against the curriculum is measured by a set of formal tests; and partly on the basis of the results of these tests, more experienced practitioners are able to apply for higher salaries.

These are controversial times. A sociological approach offers some way of making sense of this. In the classroom, pupils and teachers have to deal with all of these competing and often contradictory demands, ensuring high pupil attainment in the context of poor parental support, difficult physical contexts, while trying to obtain professional and personal satisfaction.

Both Hargreaves (1984) and Pollard (1985) recognize that teachers con-struct the world of the classroom through the employment of different teach-ing styles, but that this construction occurs in situations not of their own choosing. Furthermore, constraints on their actions require some sort of reso-lution through the decisions that they make on a daily basis. In this sense, teachers, like learners, are active constructors of their own thinking and action in the context of the immediate, institutional, and wider factors, which either aid or constrain their work. Hargreaves used the term 'coping' to describe how both teachers and pupils adapt to and indeed survive in the classroom. Coping is a creative and constructive process by which strategies are developed by both teachers and pupils to make their lives bearable and even rewarding in school. Hargreaves and Pollard developed similar models to account for the coping strategies used by both pupils and teachers in class-room learning.

Coping strategies

Hargreaves (1984) conceptualized **coping strategies** as 'active constructions of both teachers and pupils: they are adaptive and hence changing solutions to recurring daily problems'. Coping strategies are specific forms of learning strategies; but they are generalizable, and cannot be reduced to a simple set of control and response behaviours. Coping strategies are a response to the fundamentally contradictory goals of the educational system. At the classroom level, there is a common desire to educate and relate to children in the spirit of liberal individualism, and this is counter-balanced by the necessity to select and socialize children for a class-stratified society. This can be seen in the contradictory approaches of guided discovery in learning as opposed to guided choice, for instance, in the choice of qualifications and even careers.

Coping strategies develop as a response to the material restraints of the classroom. For instance, teachers and pupils have to cope with the problems of whole class subject-based learning in classrooms designed on an open plan basis for child-centred discovery approaches to learning.

Coping strategies can develop as a result of competing educational ideologies: on the part of the system, the teacher and even the pupil. Pupils have their own view of what an effective teacher is, and where a teacher's approach differs from this conception, they have to develop ways of coping. These may be by more or less deviant or compliant actions.

Coping strategies are institutionally mediated. For instance, in recent years, the expectation that pupils should do homework to support class-based learning has been enshrined in home–school agreements which are signed by parents, and in many schools also by pupils. However, in practice, completion of homework by pupils in some schools is effectively not an option for many pupils. Some pupils cope by offering a plethora of excuses for non-completion of homework, and often decide not to comply with punishments, as they know that they are practically impossible to enforce without considerable effort by the teachers involved. Therefore the situation by which some homework remains uncompleted involves a tacit collusion between teachers and pupils.

Reflection

Consider the homework policy in your school:

- How do pupils and parents respond to this?
- Is there a gap between policy and practice?
- How do you deal with pupils who do not complete homework?

Congratulations if this is not an issue for you! If it is, why is homework a problem?

Strategies for the classroom

Learning journals in primary school

One school and several teachers I know have replaced an interminable list of worksheets sent home with learning journals. Children are asked to reflect on their learning, what they have achieved, what went well, what was more difficult and where they would like to make progress.

If too structured, this becomes a vacuous activity, but careful engagement by the teacher can provide good insights into a child's view of their learning. I have seen this effectively used in both Key Stage 1 and Key Stage 2:

• A journal acts as a mirror to the writer's thoughts. It can be completed in words, pictures and diagrams.

A variation of this is the spelling journal. While many schools send lists of words home for children to learn as spellings, this is regarded as rather pointless and purposeless by many educationalists. One alternative to spelling for homework is the 'spelling journal'. Children could be asked to look for interesting words/ phrases in books and the world around them. Children can look for different patterns in the spelling of words, different families of words, different ways of making words using prefixes and suffixes. The opportunities are endless.

Coping strategies can become institutionalized depending on the response of pupils or teachers to the ways of working devised by the other. Teachers may accept a certain level of noise and off-task behaviour when they perceive that work outcomes will be achieved. Talk about the latest television soap opera by pupils and even teachers is one way that they cement their working relationship, in the face of work which is perceived as being boring (by both).

Coping strategies may be renegotiated if they are not perceived as working, by either pupils or teachers. In that sense, they are dynamic. However, the possible solutions to classroom challenges are limited by the very factors and constraints that lead to the development of classroom-coping strategies.

Coping strategies develop in a cycle, which includes classroom decision-making, pre-existing pupil/teacher coping strategies, consequences issuing from the use of such strategies, perceived success or failure of the strategies, the subjective experience of those involved, and the institutionalization of strategies. The pool of available coping strategies for both pupils and teachers is therefore dynamic, interactive and developing.

Hargreaves (1984) focused on teachers' coping strategies; however, he recognized the existence of pupil coping strategies, which were seen as influencing the teachers' work in the cycle of coping. Pollard (1985) progressed the concept of pupil coping strategies. Pollard builds on G.H. Mead's (1934) conception of 'self': recognizing the historical, social and hence biographical factors operating on both pupils and teachers in the classroom. On the one hand, pupils and teachers have to recognize the situation which must be coped with; and on the other, they must operate within frameworks which conform to images they have of themselves. Pollard defines a coping strategy as: 'a type of patterned and active adaptation to a situation by which an individual copes. It is a creative, but semi-routinised and situational means of protecting the individual's self' (1985: 155).

Like Hargreaves, Pollard (1985) recognizes that children's backgrounds (their biography) can be in conflict with the roles which they, the institution or their family expect them to fulfil. It is in this context that coping strategies develop. Pollard's analysis is stronger than that of Hargreaves, in that it recognizes and describes the phenomena which develop in the classroom. For example, Pollard highlights the concept of the 'working consensus' established at the start of the year, in which the routines, procedures and standards for the year develop. The development of the working consensus may be established through varying degrees of negotiation.

It is the interaction between teachers' and pupils' roles and biographies, and the process by which coping strategies develop which characterize the learning ethos, standards, and efficacy of the classroom. The working consensus is characterized by a number of rules and rule frames. These are tacit and taken-for-granted conventions which develop through incident and case law as the teachers and pupils come to understand each other and to define the parameters of acceptable behaviour in particular situations. Practitioners will recognize the important rule frames relating to time, place, people and activities. Pupils will behave, and learn in different ways depending on these factors. So, for example, pupils may learn differently in different subjects, different rooms, or even with different teachers (in the same rooms, doing the same activities at the same time of day!). Pupils recognize that teachers may be in a good or a bad mood, and will accept variations within unspecified ranges of teacher behaviour. However, when teachers step outside of these preconceived boundaries, pupils perceive them to be 'out of order'. Likewise a physically violent response by a pupil to teacher demands is always considered to be unacceptable by almost all pupils.

Reflection

Think of a difficult or challenging situation which you have had to deal with in school.

- How much did this relate to the transgression of your normal class routines?
- What was the reaction of your class?
- How did you re-establish or renegotiate the routines of your class?

Strategies for the classroom

Learning surveys in secondary schools

Why wait for OFSTED to ask pupils about learning in your school? Teachers can be the most self-critical of professionals but should be willing to hear pupils' thoughts on classroom learning.

I'm always uneasy about anonymous surveys and questionnaires, as they can be used to make abusive and unprofessional statements about other people. However, they can be useful in providing some feedback from learners:

- Surveys can be used to support planning for the curriculum, evaluation of teaching methods and outcomes of classroom learning.
- While progress in 'high stakes' tests seem to be one of the main ways of measuring a school's success, surely pupil satisfaction surveys offer fuller and more qualitatively valid forms of evidence.
- School councils could use a school survey to identify areas of concern in the school community.
- Blended learning offers a technological solution for understanding pupils. 'Blogs' (web-based journals) have been used very successfully as a way of engaging pupils in and out of school in a way which would not be possible during the school day.
- One secondary teacher found that her students communicated with her in a much more effective and engaging way via her 'blog' than in school.

Pollard (1985) examines a range of classroom coping strategies. Though the focus in this research is the use of learning strategies by pupils, Pollard noted that particular teacher strategies will tend to produce characteristic types of counter-strategy. It would be impossible therefore not to consider the teacher's use of strategies. Pollard highlights four main strategies used by teachers and pupils to cope with the classroom situation:

1 *Open negotiation* occurs where each party recognizes and respects the interests and concerns of the other in addition to their own. Pollard, in a very interesting account of the roles that pupils adopt in the classroom, demonstrates that different learners enter into open negotiation for different reasons. 'Gang members' may avoid this strategy, while 'goodies' may use this strategy as a seriously and openly rewarding way of dealing with the class situation. Open negotiation is associated with explanation, discussion and reasoning, on the one hand, and by confrontation avoidance, friendliness and respect on the other. It is a difficult strategy to maintain, given all of the competing and often contradictory demands for both pupils and teachers.

2   *Routinization* allows teachers to operate classroom procedures and patterns of working, which are not open to negotiation. Both teachers and pupils have to become familiar with the relatively unchanging ways that pupils may follow, if they are to be successful in the classroom. From the pupils' point of view, routinization is appealing because it allows them to please the teacher fairly easily. Pupils are then able to drift through lessons, as the means or ends to their learning are less important than the completion of the task at hand. Teachers can collude with pupil 'drifting' as this can allow them to have an easier life in the classroom, and to have a laugh with the children, which may be a major motivation for the teacher. Drifting can be counter-productive from the teacher's point of view, when standards drop, key benchmarks are not met and senior managers start to ask questions about the effectiveness of their teaching.

3   *Manipulation* involves getting the pupils to want what the teacher wants: a transformation of the pupils' interests at hand by presenting work or the classroom setting itself in a positive light. Though much effective teaching relies on this approach, it is in effect an exercising of teacher power and thus involves a form of manipulation. Appeal to pupil loyalty is an example of manipulation. Of course, this might involve the pupils manipulating the teacher: for example, by appealing to the teacher for extensions to homework deadlines, sometimes in emotionally charged requests involving tears. Manipulation requires well-developed social and communication skills in the teacher. Where the teacher lacks these skills, the pupil may meet manipulation by the teacher with evasion. As discussed earlier, homework is one issue which some pupils may cope with by simply not doing it: evasion can be the pupils' response to teacher manipulation.

4   *Domination* involves the use of the expected power differential between teachers and pupils. Quite simply, teachers can deny pupils certain activities if they do not do as the teacher says: 'If you don't finish your work, you can't go out to play.' Some children will simply conform to the expectations of the teacher when faced with such an approach, even if this goes against their interests at hand. However, this tends to result in the withdrawal of the pupil from the teacher, and a lack of engagement on the part of the pupil. Another defensive strategy by the pupil is refusal in which they retreat into the protection of their peer group as a means of protecting their interests at hand and their dignity. Where pupils are being taught in larger groups or in whole class activities, the balance of power may be seen to shift to the pupils, and in these circumstances a more active form of rebellion may appear to be more viable. This is sometimes present in

classes where the teacher is seen to be particularly 'soft' or unskilled; or where the teacher is unfamiliar with classroom practices, as in the case of a supply or trainee teacher.

Pollard (1985) highlights the relative realms of influence prevalent in the range of classroom coping strategies. For instance, *manipulation–evasion* and *domination–rebellion* are relatively unilateral acts. *Open negotiation*, on the other hand, implies a consensual approach. The most dynamic evolving and commonly used strategies (*routinization–drifting* and *manipulation–evasion*) involve a struggle between the interests at hand of the teacher and pupils. The classroom struggle involves the developing profile of strategies used by teacher and pupils. The teacher leaves the pupils enough room to develop strategies to adapt to the challenges of the classroom, and the pupils develop strategies within the boundaries of acceptability of the teacher and wider expectations of the educational system.

Interestingly, Pollard notes that the different roles which boys and girls believe are expected of their gender will be important factors of influence on the coping strategies used by both teachers and pupils. For instance, girls are said to use more subtle forms of coping, and more effective communication skills predispose them to use negotiating skills more effectively than boys. Boys, on the other hand, may be more disposed to use open rebellion as a coping strategy, particularly if they see themselves as gang members. By exerting power over the teacher, they increase their standing in the peer group.

Pollard (1982) suggested that coping strategies are the forms of action taken by individuals to satisfy their 'interests at hand'. Pollard's work emphasized the role of the teacher and the sometimes contradictory requirements of the curriculum, school and pupils which results in the development of coping strategies in the teacher. These may be targeted at improving their ability to teach at one level, or at merely aiding them to survive in the classroom. To understand the concept of 'interests at hand', I will explain the concept of 'self'. This term is used freely by many educationalists in their description of educational issues (self-regulation, self-interest, self-motivated, etc.), but what does it really mean?

The self

A key concept underpinning the work of sociologists like Pollard (1985) and psychologists like Dweck (1999), is the notion of the 'self'. This can be traced back to G.H. Mead (1934: 173):

The essence of the self, as we have said, is cognitive: it lies in the internalised conversation of gestures, which constitute thinking, or in terms of which thought or reflection proceeds. And hence the origin and the foundations of the self, like those of thinking, are social.

An important feature of the concept of self is in the subjective ('I') and the objective ('me'). The 'I' represents our own internal view of ourselves, and the 'me' represents our reactions to the attitudes and perception that others have for us. This distinction is very important for the analysis of learning strategies and self-regulation. In Dweck's (1999) model, the development of self-theories mediates interactions with the learning situation. Mead's distinction allows us to recognize that it is both our own view of ourselves, and our views about how others perceive us that actually contribute to these theories. Here again, both cognitive and motivational features are interdependent. Personality and temperament may be important factors in driving our view of ourselves, but this view is still a personal construct driven by cognition.

I would like to suggest in this book that learners develop a range of strategies to support their own learning. These are called self-support learning strategies. These are the affective, social and cognitive strategies which pupils use to support their development in new areas of learning.

Hewitt (2004) provides examples of how pupils in four secondary schools used learning strategies to 'cope' with their class setting. This setting is conceived of as a network of connected and interdependent factors, such as the work; their relations with other pupils and the teacher; and the often conflicting requirements of the curriculum compared to their own interests and perceived needs.

Network of interdependencies

The bridging of the gap between more overtly psychological and sociological models of learning rests in the understanding that the self exists on the physical, mental and social levels, arguably also on a moral level. Thus, a model of self-regulation must recognize that learning is never entirely independent. In fact, it always exists in a complex network of interdependencies: an interconnected context involving physical, mental and social factors.

Effective learning involves the ability to function well in the network of interdependencies associated with the learner.

The active learner employs an appropriate range of self-support learning strategies to extract an appropriate level of support from the physical, cognitive and social environment. The following are important:

- *Physical resources* such as classroom reference materials such as dictionaries, thesauruses, encyclopaedias, classroom displays and resources beyond the class such as the Internet, libraries and the media.

- *Cognitive support* such as advice from able peers and the teacher about solving a problem.
- *Social support* (such as the development of peer group status that can come from working with other learners).

Terms such as 'effective self-regulated and dependent' learning capture something of the role of learners in a learning journey though they are somewhat contradictory in tone. On the one hand, learning involves the learner mastering a new skill or coming to an understanding of a new concept; with the support of more able others. A learner is dependent on others for support until they are able to regulate the new area of learning without support in the future, hence, self-regulation. From this perspective learning always takes place in a social setting. Understanding the learning process is both enlightening for researchers, but also provides some insight for the classroom practitioner as to how they might support pupils in school. What is the evidence that learners use strategies to support their learning in school?

Pupils interviewed in Hewitt (2004) provided some interesting perspectives. On first consideration, they thought that the successful independent learner was one who could use a range of strategies to work on their own. In some cases, the qualities of the independent learner were focused more on high levels of confidence and the ability to work hard (high effort). This view was very much confirmed by their teachers, who thought that a major part of their role was to instil confidence in their pupils. With confidence, the teachers felt that pupils would be able to learn effectively. Neither pupils nor teachers were very specific about the nature of learning strategies and therefore the child's role in learning independently.

As the research progressed, a developing counter-viewpoint became prominent: this had developed from the observation and interview data. Since learning always takes place in a social setting, it can be argued that no learning is truly independent. The conception of an independent learner working 'solo', therefore moved towards a dependent learner working effectively, in a 'socially' adept way: in relation to the teacher and other pupils. Pupils and teachers clearly felt that the most effective learner was the one who could work effectively at the cognitive as well as the social level. Furthermore, there was some discussion about the role of confidence and motivation in the 'independent learner'.

Pupils were quick to point out that despite being very successful, some learners actually had little confidence in their own abilities. However, they were clearly motivated and there is substantial evidence to suggest that effective learners are able to manufacture opportunities for positive reinforcement of their learning by both peers and teachers. Clarificatory questions can operate at two levels. On the one hand, pupils know how to extract support from teachers: for instance, in clarifying the task, language and expectations of an activity. On the other, they are able to gain positive feedback from the teacher in respect of their attempt to perform any one activity. Such a strategy is therefore important in enabling the 'independent learner' to maintain motivation for learning: a contribution to both the cognitive and affective dimensions. This exists at the level of a lesson task or indeed in the longer term, for exam success.

Some pupils clearly value learning more than some others do. The evidence from both male and female pupils suggested that there was a significant pressure against valuing learning. Effective and 'independent learners' had made a moral judgement that learning was not 'uncool', because they could see beyond the short-term gains of popularity within the peer group, towards the potential long-term benefits of a successful education. This is a moral judgement, and very much conforms to Kozeki's (1985) view that while cognitive, affective and social strategies are important for the successful learner, so is a moral dimension.

To summarize, then, self-support strategies include cognitive, affective, social and moral features. They are supportive of the learner's own development: often directly in the short term, but sometimes indirectly in the longer term. If we move to a conception of the effective learner as one who is essentially dependent on the other participants, then it is clear to see that a social network of dependencies exists in any classroom. Effective learners support each other, and this mutual support builds up social credit with the peer group. Several of the pupils (particularly males) suggested that they will respond positively and be supportive to the ideas of peers within the group, as that will result in future support from those same individuals. We are here moving towards a definition of the social construction of the 'self', in the sense proposed by Demetriou (2000), following from James (1892) and Markus and Wurf (1987). On the one hand, the self exists at the intrapersonal level, but it also exists on the interpersonal level. According to Markus and Wurf (1987), the working self-concept can impact on information processing, motivation and self-regulation at the intrapersonal level.

At the interpersonal level, working self-concept can influence social perception, partner choice, interaction strategies and reactions to feedback. James (1892) suggested that one element of the self was the social self. It is this notion, which is encapsulated within the concept of 'self-support learning'. Of course, strategies are used by individuals to support their own learning, but importantly, effective learners are able to recognize that supporting others can have a powerfully positive impact on others' perceptions of themselves, and in the longer term on their own learning. Support for others can be mutually beneficial:

> Social life necessitates that individuals interact with both the physical environment and each other . . . It creates a mental environment in

addition to or on top of the actual environment. This entails the construction of a sense of personal identity or self as the central engine of self-understanding and self-regulation.

(Demetriou 2000: 212)

Ultimately, do we want learners or learning which is independent? This may seem to be a strange point given the focus on learning strategies in this book. However, we could always say that the most effective learners are those who are able to take from the available resources (physical, teacher or peer support) to enable them to achieve levels of skills and understanding which would be impossible if they were to carry out the activities entirely on their own. The following observation suggests that affective factors such as confidence in one's own ability are seen by pupils as an important element of effective learning:

> M— is really clever and got level 8s in her KS3 SATs, but she hasn't got a lot of confidence in herself as a learner.
>
> (Pupil)

Ethnographic approaches to investigating classroom learning are absolutely essential if we are to come to a greater understanding of what constitutes relevant, purposeful and challenging learning. As Britton said: 'We build what is for each other a representation of the world and at the same time is to each other a representation of a different individuality, another self' (1970: 150). So what does this mean for the individual learner in school? This will be the focus of the next chapter.

Summary of implications for the teacher

Underachievement can develop where school and home culture are significantly different

- Important values of the home and school community may not be mutually reinforced.

Lifelong learning starts with a child's first encounter with the education system

- Children's learning in primary and secondary schools is merely one, be it very important, part of the continuum of 'lifelong learning'.
- Demotivated primary and secondary age learning could have a long-term impact on future lifelong learners.

Engage pupils more actively in planning and implementing the curriculum

- Learners take greater responsibility for their learning in such settings. Motivation for learning is increased and the learners have a more positive view of themselves.
- Activities should be personally meaningful to the learner, that is, engaging and relevant in a way that assists them in their own meaning making.

Teachers and pupils develop coping strategies to make their lives bearable and rewarding in school

- Coping strategies are dynamic and quick to change according to classroom events.

Confidence is not necessarily correlated with ability

- Some learners, despite being high achievers, have little self-confidence; while others have high levels of confidence but do not achieve well in school.

Class management and groupings can be influenced by the gender of learners

- According to some teachers and pupils, girls tend to choose friends of similar academic abilities, whereas boys tend to choose friends of differing academic abilities.

Learning involves the ability to function in a network of interdependencies associated with the learner

- These include cognitive, physical and especially social dimensions to the classroom and school context.

4 Learning strategies and the individual learner

I think they [the pupils] should have more autonomy than they've got. It's been my experience that children have learnt more when they're interested in something. Some of the topics that we are forced to teach are really not that interesting for 10- to 11-year olds. For the time we spend doing them, they don't get enough out of it.

(Year 5/6 teacher, quoted in McNess et al. 2003: 133)

This chapter will help you to:

- develop an understanding of the learner as an individual;
- understand the different types of classroom self-support learning strategies;
- identify ways of developing self-regulated learning in class.

Wood (1998) suggests that educational success of pupils in school depends on the learner developing self-regulation in various key areas. In some cases the strategies for regulation may be subject-specific and in other cases, they may be of a more generic nature. Self-support strategies operate in the same way. For instance, 'clarificatory' strategies enable learners to obtain more information about a task or activity in order to resolve a misconception or confusion about how it should be carried out: pupils in school B asked the teacher how much time they had to complete a written newspaper report. This is a generic self-support strategy, which could be used in any subject to clarify issues related to learning.

We have already explored in Chapter 3 the response of learners and teachers to the complex social setting within which learning takes place. When the frequently complex and conflicting demands of the classroom cannot be resolved, then the response is to develop coping strategies to deal with the situation. I suggested that learners can adopt learning strategies to support their learning. These are explained in the following framework.

A framework of self-support learning strategies

Figure 4.1 explains the theoretical framework within which this research has been developed. *Self-support learning strategies are the affective, social and cognitive learning strategies which pupils use to support their development in the classroom.* Figure 4.1 shows the various categories of self-support strategies as a mind map. Each category represents a group or cluster of strategies which have been analysed on the basis of observations, interviews and checks made with pupils and teachers in a range of secondary schools. Any analysis of learning strategies is problematic: should an observation of learning be classified as one category as opposed to another? You will be able to judge for yourself whether you agree with the following classification of learning strategies. As a researcher, one must strive for reliability and validity in the analysis of classroom reality (Kvale 2002). The best way to achieve that is through establishing a secure dialogue with the classroom players (namely teachers and their pupils). Over a period of four years in four different secondary schools, the analysis of self-support learning strategies involved a constant reflection on the evidence and how the analysis was seen by teachers and pupils. For primary colleagues I believe that the analysis is indeed plausible, although I would argue that every classroom, every school and every phase of education is likely to have a distinctive profile of self-strategies present in the classroom. Classroom and school contexts have a direct impact on the profile of learning in every setting!

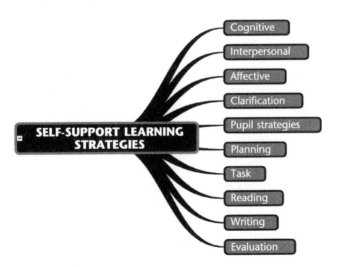

Figure 4.1   Framework of self-support learning strategies

Reflection

Think about the various phases (planning, implementation and evaluation) of an activity for both learners and teachers:

- What are the implications for teachers and learners of self-support learning strategies?
- While the teacher might be anxious to make learning objectives and success criteria explicit for learners, would it not also be very helpful for learners if teachers and learners thought explicitly about self-support learning strategies to facilitate the learning?

There is no guarantee that this will lead to perfection, but it surely makes sense to consider in explicit terms *how to* learn as well as *what to* learn.

Strategies for the classroom

Five fingers of the learning hand

Whatever the age-range you work with, this activity approach can help children in any learning activity.

Look at the fingers of one hand. Each finger represents a question to ask yourself in any activity. It will help to think about the questions before, during and after any activity.

Thumb:	WHAT do you have to do?
	Think about the main thing you will learn in an activity.
First finger:	WHEN do you have to complete an activity?
	Think about how best to use the time available.
Second finger:	WHO can help complete an activity?
	Think about how you will work with other people or ask for help from others if there is a problem.
Third finger:	HOW do you complete an activity?
	Think about what order and the best way to complete an activity.
Fourth finger:	WHY should you complete an activity?
	Think before you start the activity, what you personally and others will gain from the learning in an activity. This is the most important as it will help you to stay motivated.

It is important to recognize that self-support learning strategies may be present at almost any point in a lesson. A summary of each group of strategies is provided below to explain the framework.

Cognitive self-support learning strategies

- Explicit consideration of problems encountered in learning.
- Processes for making decisions in pairs or groups, with given alternatives.
- Development of 'creative' responses to a task, by elaborating or expanding on others' ideas.
- Development of thinking through structured course such as 'Somerset Thinking Skills' course.

Interpersonal self-support learning strategies

- Teacher-to-pupil, pupil-to-teacher and pupil-to-pupil discussion, direction, and joking.
- Continuum of agreement to disagreement, informal to formal.
- Group processes/roles (leaders and jokers) vs learning in pairs vs individual working.
- Organization of learners in social, and physical manner in groups, pairs or individuals.
- Social interaction (off-task chat and joking) for academic and emotional ends.

Affective self-support learning strategies

- State and process in development of ambience, trust and motivation in classroom by both pupils and teacher.
- Continuum from 'relaxed' to 'strict' class atmosphere.
- Teacher and pupil strategies for resolution of previously 'bad' class reputations.
- Class atmosphere developed by few individuals acting in roles (joker, clown, rebel and leader).

Clarification self-support learning strategies

- Strategies and processes by which pupils question aspects of classroom activities (content, quantity, method and linguistic features).
- Ways in which pupils and teacher resolve ambiguities, misunderstandings and seek to gain reassurance for ways of acting and learning in class.

Pupil self-support learning strategies

- Conscious and explicitly used strategies to support own and others' learning: through analogy, diagrams, summarizing, reviewing, improvisation, rephrasing and use of classroom tools to develop understanding.
- Use of basic writing skills, role play improvisation and presentation.

Planning self-support learning strategies

- Spoken, written methods and processes including diagrams and notes to develop content, vocabulary, quantity and quality of the given task.
- Planning involves comprehension of the task and the resources available to the learner.

Task self-support learning strategies

- Pupils' and teachers' perception of the nature, process and success of a learning activity.
- Tasks in different modes: speaking, reading, writing, personal, social, emotional and linguistic.
- Tasks involve assessment of initial task analysis, identification of roles, resources and methods for task completion (organizing and negotiating with others), evaluation of task completion (in relation to targets or perceived expectations).

Reading self-support learning strategies

- Methods for reading a range of texts: fiction, non-fiction, play scripts, work-sheets, extracts (in a lesson) and whole texts (over a sequence of lessons).
- Reading routines: aloud, silently, in a group or in pairs.
- Annotation to develop active reading methods.
- Narrative structures all important for reading: characters, setting as well as lexical and emotional features of the text.

Writing self-support learning strategies

- Skills of composition and transcription of fiction and non-fiction texts: focused on narrative structures, format, language and vocabulary choice.
- Group, paired and individual writing.

- Writing routines: dictation, drafting and reviewing.
- Collaborative writing in series and in parallel.

Evaluation self-support learning strategies

- Reflection on features of learning and behaviour: text, own/peer performance and task (teacher expectations, content, quantity, quality, method and performance against targets).

Strands of self-support learning strategies

Self-support learning strategies incorporate three strands: affective, cognitive and social. If a moral dimension is seen to be distinct from these, then this constitutes a fourth strand. Examples are given below to illustrate the framework.

'Interpersonal' self-support learning strategies

The 'interpersonal' cluster is seen as a cluster of self-support strategies centred on the social features of the classroom situation, in whole class, group or paired situations. These include use of communication strategies (such as discussion, disagreement and making suggestions to others), the use of directing strategies (such as directing attention to specific aspects of a task or text), the use of organization strategies (associated with working in groups or pairs), and especially the use of social interaction strategies (such as the use of humour to dissipate stress, and to encourage self-motivation for a task).

Pupil 1: I think it's only fair if K— does the first question because she hasn't read.
Pupil 2: Shut up.
Pupil 1: This is group work you know [said jokily].
Pupil 2: I'll go with that then.
Pupil 1: Let's move on, then. Get on with the work. The matter in hand.

(Year 9 lesson)

Shortly after the above discussion of who will be doing what in a group activity, one of the boys carries on talking but in the style of 'Ali G' (a TV comic character of the time). When asked why he had done that, the pupil explained:

Yeah, C— often does that and we have a laugh, coz sometimes it's boring, That's how we get though the lesson.

(Year 9 pupil)

Arguably one could say that this social interaction is marginal, and should not be seen as part of the 'interpersonal' cluster of self-support learning strategies. This is problematic in analysing learning strategies. For instance, how direct must the impact on learning be to be considered for inclusion in the 'interpersonal' cluster of self-support strategies? I believe here that the marginalization of social interactions is a superficial view of their role in learning. Not only does all learning take place within a social context, but also humour, teasing, sarcasm, joking and word play are important in developing cohesion within the peer group (Pollard 1998). Remember that the pupils in school D said that this helped them 'get through the work'.

Pupils suggested it was easier to 'get more ideas when you start off' than if 'you did it on your own'. In the following extract a pupil suggests that one strategy for planning and for preliminary drafting of work involves writing down all the ideas of a group in response to questions, and identify which ideas are the 'best'. The middle item relates more to the roles adopted by pupils in a group.

> Researcher: What about working in groups? Is it easier to work in groups?
> Pupil 1: Yeah it's easier because in a group there are more ideas, and when you start off. People have ideas and then other people expand on them, and you get better ideas than if you did it on your own.
> Researcher: Did you find that when you were working in the groups did you appoint a spokesman? Because I know that Miss C– suggested this.
> Pupil 1: Well, I sorted the group out and there was a girl who is quite good at that sort of thing and we shared being the spokesman.
> Researcher: What about you?
> Pupil 2: I sort of wrote the questions out. That we had in the group and then we all wrote down our ideas to see who had the best answers for the group.

In order for these strategies to operate, pupils must have knowledge and understanding of the principal features of the classroom. 'Interpersonal' self-support strategies require knowledge and understanding of:

- *language*: for example, the linguistic structures and vocabulary associated with whole class, group and paired communications;
- *learning*: for example, the principles by which effective learning takes place, which includes an understanding of the potential benefits of working with others rather than on your own;
- *teaching strategies*: for example, knowing the rules of interaction with teachers, and understanding their role in the learning process;

- *targets*: for example, the nature of time, quantity, quality and method-related targets.

The 'interpersonal' cluster of self-support strategies can be further situated in the context of 'gender' (for example, girls were, generally, said to work in pairs of similar abilities, whereas boys were, generally, said to work in larger groups of mixed ability status, when given the choice by their teacher); and the 'school' (many schools said that they had too few resources to encourage the appropriate use of resources such as information books, dictionaries and thesauruses). The latter was an important overall contextual category, as it illustrated the impact of exams and the ongoing controversies about the nature of English as a subject. These will clearly have an impact on the range of self-support strategies that are favoured in class. Clearly, if there are no exams in speaking and listening, and English is constituted more as reading and writing, then the opportunities for using 'interpersonal' self-support learning strategies may be reduced.

Pupils and teachers confirmed that the strategies actually observed and analysed were typical (be it a sub-set) of the overall cluster. At the time some pupils were reflecting on my analysis of their lessons, they had just completed a short period of work experience. This had changed their perception of the priorities in learning. As an aside they said that they felt exams and GCSEs were less relevant than they had already said at the time of the original data collection. However, additionally they had developed the view that: 'In the workplace you have to stand up for yourself a lot more (than in school).' Consequently they felt that their experience of the work placement had focused their attention on the importance of self-support strategies of a social and interpersonal nature. Presumably strategies of an 'interpersonal' nature would allow one to engage with colleagues in the workplace to develop a positive working relationship. Furthermore, these strategies would allow the worker to use their initiative while working with others. As they said, 'At work they give you a task and you have to get on with it.'

'Affective' self-support learning strategies

The 'affective' cluster of self-support strategies is focused on aspects of motivation and emotional support within the classroom. This analysis links to the work of Dweck (1999) who says that 'emotions are importantly tied into cognition'. This is illustrated by the following interview comment from a pupil in school D: 'We usually get ideas as a group. And then one person takes the lead. That tends to be me. Because I'm a bit more confident than other people.' Confidence is seen by the pupil as enabling him to take the lead in a group in terms of developing ideas. The notion of 'confidence' appears to be employed by pupils and teachers to denote the emotional characteristics and strategies that are necessary to support learning. This is a problematic notion and it will be further explored in the following section. In the first example above, the pupil in school D said that he tended to lead a group, because he had 'more confidence than others'. The following extract from an interview with the teacher in school D exemplifies one aspect of the 'affective' cluster:

> Yeah. I find that across the whole school not just in this class. You always need to be giving confidence and praising them all the time saying, 'Yes that's fine', 'You can do it.' You know.
>
> (Teacher)

Here the teacher explains that 'confidence' and 'praise' are necessary features of more successful learning. By implication, she suggests that without confidence and praise the pupils are less likely to achieve the learning expected by the teachers.

According to the pupils' views of learning ('cool' or 'uncool'), they may employ 'affective' strategies, which contribute to a positive or a negative classroom ambience. Many teachers explained that they had had to work very hard to turn around classes, who were seen by themselves and by other teachers as being 'bad'. Clearly, they worked very hard to engender a positive class atmosphere, but this would not have occurred without the participation of the pupils. When a group of poorly behaved pupils had been in the class in previous years, some individuals had adopted an 'anti-learning' attitude, despite the fact that they had significant potential to do well in the classroom. This corresponds closely to the coping strategies explained by Pollard (1985). In Pollard's conception, pupils can adopt certain roles in the classroom, as a way of coping with the often contradictory and competing priorities (of the teacher, the curriculum and the peer group). Of the roles described by Pollard (1985), there were clear examples of 'goodies' and 'jokers', in addition to a category of 'leaders'. For instance, a pupil in school D explained how different pupils took the lead in a class activity in English depending on the pupils' assessment of the prevailing expectation in the class:

> He does sometimes, but we're not always in the same group. Michael takes the lead sometimes. But if it's more serious I'll take the lead. If it's more jokey Michael or Chris will take the lead.

I believe that while teachers have expectations about the classroom ambiance, 'class atmosphere' is very much also constructed by pupils. Pupils use 'affective' self-support learning strategies to construct the class atmosphere (Pollard 1998).

Pupils in school D were quite emphatic about the role of class 'leader' which had been adopted by one of the pupils to secure his own learning as well the learning of others in the class. Though the pupil had been elected as a form representative, this individual considered his role to be much more extensive than just that of representing his class at meetings. He would become involved in settling disputes between individuals (away from the teacher), as well as encouraging others when they were struggling in class.

'Motivation' was also considered to be part of the 'affective' cluster of strategies. Motivation is a complex concept, but for the purposes of this analysis it is considered that this involves strategies which help pupils to identify the emotional factors which influence the attainment of certain goals (Dweck 1999). A pupil in school D articulated motivation for activities that he considered to be 'real life':

> It depends what lesson it is and what piece of work you're doing. People at the moment like learning because it's real life and people enjoy doing it. But if it's about books that people think are a bit sad then they won't enjoy doing it.

The teacher in school D explained what she thought was motivating for pupils:

> I mean, you're not here because you're enjoying yourselves. You maybe don't want to be here. But you may as well be here and get good results and get a good job. And get good money that's what you're in this for. That's the line I take with them because that's what they can relate to.

At one level, it is quite a stark expression to say that 'pupils do not come to school to enjoy themselves'. At another level, the teacher seems to suggest that pupils are motivated by more instrumental goals. This view is not quite congruent with that of the pupil interviewed from her class. He felt that pupils were particularly motivated by some of the work in English (for instance, a unit of work on the execution of Derek Bentley) because it 'related to real life'. However, he did say that many pupils perceived that by working hard they would get good results in their exams and this would ultimately help them to obtain better jobs later in life. It is possible that pupils could have different motivations (short-term and long-term).

Knowledge of and an understanding of the classroom setting and routines underpin this particular use of learning strategies:

- *learning*: achieving a balance of motivation, effort, organization, social ability and confidence to encourage effective learning;
- *teaching strategies*: understanding the forms of pedagogical support that the teacher can offer;

- *targets*: in the short term, meeting the expectations of the teacher in the class; and in the longer term, meeting the expectations of the school in respect of exam performance.

The role of the 'leader' is an extremely sophisticated one, in the sense that he or she has to steer a pathway through the expectations of both the teacher and the peer group. Too learning-focused and they risk being derided as 'swots'. Too peer-focused and they risk deviating from the expectations of the teacher. It is clear in the example of school D that 'humour' was the way that enabled learners and teachers to facilitate the passageway through classroom learning. So when the pupil carried out an activity entirely in the 'voice' of Ali G (an alternative comic TV persona) in school D, this was because it allowed them to carry out the learning task (meeting teacher expectations), while 'having a laugh' (meeting peer expectations). 'School' contextual features and routines such as homework provided pupils with the context within which they could reinforce the relationships with the peer group, by supporting each other in the completion of tasks. Year 9 SATs, GCSEs and the transition into Year 10 and entry into Key Stage 4 were seen as a 'rites of passage' by both teachers and pupils: though pupils were less motivated to do well in Year 9 SATs, exam success was an important motivation. This provided pupils with the opportunities to gain praise from the teacher. As previously mentioned, gender was an important contextual factor: especially so, since one of the schools had used this as a way of organizing classes.

'Task' self-support learning strategies

The 'task' cluster of self-support strategies involves analysing a learning activity at the outset, to verify the expectations and targets set by the teacher, identifying methods for organizing the task (including roles for other learners, and how available resources can be used to support), and assessment of task completion. This is marked by cognitive (assessment of learning outcomes and objectives), social (resources include those of other learners) and affective factors (making a judgement as to whether non-task 'jokes' and 'messing around' are required, in order to make the task palatable).

Teachers were asked to explain how they thought the ideal learner would approach a task, and to describe this in relation to the best learners in their classes. The teacher in school D (in the above extract from an observation on 21 June 2001), for instance, highlighted the pupils' previous experiences of carrying out a role-play presentation prior to the development of a 'news report' role-play about the Derek Bentley case. In essence, the teacher in school B was scaffolding what the ideal learner would be able to do on their own: following the analysis of class learning sequences in Edwards and Mercer (1987). The teacher in school B suggested that ideal learners would not only be able to analyse the requirements of any particular task, but that they should be able to reflect on their own skills and experiences to identify the best way of approaching an activity:

> Someone I would class as a fairly independent learner would be that they would sort of digest the task itself so the initial instructions to the task, and then as there are some examples in here they do tend to think about, their own kind of ideas on that task. And there are some of them in here who are quite good at thinking about their own ability within that kind of task and they're fairly hooked on to their strengths and weaknesses so you tend to say within a group that they will start to sort form around their strengths.
>
> One of the last pieces of work we did was based on an advertising campaign so it included doing some designs and adverts for a new product of their choice. When they went into groups that was totally independent. This is what you must produce at the end, go away and, come back with something and present it to the rest of the class and that was fairly telling in terms of what an independent learner would do because within their groups they very quickly organized who was kind of good at what and where their strengths lay, and the individually they then thought about how much they would expect themselves to kind of produce. And they were also fairly good at watching other groups as well, you can see them looking at, for example, what M– is doing because they do see M– as the brightest person in the class.
>
> So they kind of gauge themselves, 'Well, if M–'s doing six sides of A4, then probably I could do about four; although they're doing the same kinds of things they'll watch other learners and see where they're at. They'll think, 'Well, S–'s about the same level as me, if S–'s done that much, then I'll do that, but generally, I don't know, it's really difficult to think about, do think about it, that's the kind of learner that I hope that I manage to produce. Someone who's fairly independent and someone who will be able to do things for themselves. Whether it works I don't really know but that's kind of generally what hopefully the classroom's set up to do.
>
> (Teacher)

In fact, the above extract exemplifies the social nature of self-support learning strategies. In terms of the task, the teacher suggests that the independent learner not only has awareness of their own strengths but also of those of other people within a group:

> There are some of them in here who are quite good at thinking about their own ability within/that kind of task and they're fairly hooked on

to their strengths and weaknesses so you tend to say within a group that they will start to sort from around their strengths.

(Teacher)

Likewise, more independent learners will be able to learn from other groups: 'they were also fairly good at watching other groups.'

Knowledge and understanding of 'learning' processes are of considerable use in completing any task: teachers often used the start of lessons to refer pupils to previous tasks, so that they may think about the processes involved in completing similar activities. This could be seen as focusing pupils on the corpus of task completion templates. Tasks are completed in different modes of English (speaking and listening, reading and writing) and therefore demand different understanding of language: features found in spoken as opposed to written text types. Teachers in schools B, C and D made a great deal of the importance of Standard English for formal settings, purposes and audiences. Pupils were quite sensitive to the use of non-standard English, including 'swearing'. Teachers gave pupils advice as to which swear words could be used according to the context.

In school D, pupils were allowed to use a selection of swear words in the dialogue associated with a role-play based on the murder of a policeman, in the Derek Bentley case. In structuring the method by which a task was completed (however informally this form took), an understanding of the teacher strategies for support was clearly important in plotting the resources to support the completion of a task: the girls of school C said that in drafting their descriptive narrative writing, they knew that if they got stuck in the middle of drafting, they could always turn to the teacher for some help in completing or rewriting sentences.

Teachers acknowledged the complexity of tasks confronting learners:

- How would pupils achieve the given outcome?
- What are the specific parts of the task?
- How will the parts be sequenced/structured?
- How long will pupils spend on each part of the task?
- Depending on the nature of the task, learners will need to consider aspects of text: for instance, text structure and content.
- How will the pupils know when they have successfully completed the task?

These elements are evidenced in the following extract from an observation of school D, in which the teacher introduces the task, and requests that the pupils organize themselves, prior to carrying out an assessed spoken presentation:

Teacher: What I would like please is to organize your groups. You don't need to move around. But you need to sit down and have a run through because in ten minutes I'd like to see the first group. In 10 minutes. You haven't got time to rearrange the room.

Pupil: We've got to think about how we're gonna do it. So you start you introduce yourself. Then you ask me and C–'s point of view on that bit. Then he gets a phone call. I'll do four points. He'll go through them and then he'll get a phone call. And you'll get more violent.

Understanding of 'targets' gives pupils insight into the time, quality and methodological constraints on the completion of the activity: a marker against which they assess their work towards the completion. The reality of assessment of completion, as has already been discussed, is not quite as sophisticated as is recorded in some psychological theories. For instance, pupils' conceptions of completion were fairly limited.

- Pupils in school A thought that completion occurred at the point when they 'got bored'.
- Pupils in school B thought that completion occurred at the point of filling all the space on a piece of paper.

'School' contextual features had a direct impact on the way learners tackled 'tasks'. Resources for learners are an important consideration when completing any task: in some of the schools, dictionaries, thesauruses and other information resources were freely available. In other schools, teachers acted as gatekeepers to the resources. The books were locked away in classroom resource cupboards, so pupils therefore did not bother asking for them. Many teachers felt that they did not have enough resources, and this had a serious impact on the ability of children to support their own learning.

The teacher and pupils in school D introduced the notion of 'risk' (previously referred to in an interview reproduced below) to the discussion of the 'task' cluster.

> The trouble is they're also the kind of students who also are very unwilling to get things wrong and they're very unwilling to take risks with things because of that, that's where the idea of them having much more independence in terms of the tasks that they can do, that's the reason that I sort of set that up with them.
>
> (Teacher)

They both considered that every task carries a certain level of risk for an individual, which is specific to that person. Whereas one person may find doing a spoken activity in front of the class to be very challenging and therefore involve a great deal of risk, others may perceive the level of risk involved with the same task to be much lower, if not non-existent. While the thought of attempting a 'risky' activity could mean possible ridicule for one person, it might present another with the stage on which he or she can perform and therefore receive the plaudits of the class. What the teacher and pupils do to create a positive class climate ('affective' cluster of strategies) can diminish the level of risk, which pupils associate with the classroom. Pupils in school C, for instance, said that they preferred group tasks because 'people felt more comfortable within a group'. In a whole class setting, if you said something in the class others (especially boys) would ' take the mickey' out of you, so it was not worth the risk. We can see here, therefore, that like many other examples of learning strategies, the 'task' cluster is very much interlinked to the 'affective' cluster.

> People feel more comfortable working in a group. You get more ideas and people are more likely to have a go because they're not so worried about people taking the mickey.
>
> (Pupil)

By employing strategies to develop confidence ('affective' cluster), pupils could feel more comfortable about undertaking a task (using 'task' cluster strategies), because they viewed the task as being less 'risky'. This reinforces the argument made that clusters of self-support strategies are very much inter-related.

'Evaluation' self-support learning strategies

The 'evaluation' cluster of strategies is linked to others. For instance, evaluation of task completion has been mentioned in the last example. Evaluation here can be sub-categorized into teacher-prompted evaluation, performance (during task) evaluation and text evaluation.

A teacher explains how 'end of unit evaluation' involves pupils choosing from a number of targets, which she writes on the board.

> This is where you need to improve. Well, in fact, I ask them what they think that they did well. This a strength, this is an area of weakness. And what they'll then do is write in a target in their planner. And then they'll write in a strategy for how they're going to deal with it.

This is not an example of 'during task' evaluation as this occurs following a teacher's prompt. However, it is very interesting to note that the teacher uses the word 'strategy'. Pupils write in a 'target' in their 'planners' to indicate how they will take action to improve on areas for development. The teacher uses the terms 'strategy' and 'target' interchangeably here. The teacher says that pupils can choose from a given list of targets but there is no evidence to suggest that a list of strategies is given. Is it that the teacher requires evaluation of learning, but with no suggestion of the strategies, which pupils might use to respond to those targets?

Performance evaluation involved pupils either as individuals, pairs, groups or the whole class considering their own or others' performance, and making an evaluation against specified criteria. In other cases, the teacher prompted evaluation. For example, in an assessment task by the teacher in school D pupils carried out role-play presentations about the case of Derek Bentley. Pupils had to observe others and evaluate their performance in terms of the use of Standard English, the quality of their role-play, and the fluency of their presentation.

> Teacher: Yes, it was good, wasn't it? OK, thank you, boys, that was very good. Let's just get back to your seats.
> [next group presentation interspersed by applause]
> Teacher: Comments, please.
> Pupil: Matthew answered very emotionally.

In the above extract, there is a pattern of teacher questions followed by pupil answers. In some cases, the answers are stimulated by an instruction ('Comments, please'), and in others by a question ('Anything else?'). How do we know that the pupils' responses amount to evaluation? Phrases like 'It's good' hardly constitute detailed analysis of the classroom task. Is the pupil merely filling a space in the classroom interaction between teacher and pupils when they say this? Are they just saying what the teacher wants to hear? If the response to the initial question was 'That was absolutely awful', this could not only antagonize the teacher but other pupils in the class. In this situation, pupils are passing comments on each other's news report presentations. If they were to pass negative comments on someone else's presentation, it could be that they might be the target of negative comments from the original recipient of their comments.

Pupils, in general, were very positive about the performances by peers; though there was some debate as to whether pupils were only positive so that they might receive similar approbation themselves. There seemed to be an unwritten rule that pupils should not be sarcastic about the work of others. When, in school D, sarcastic comments were made by boys of a girl's presentation, this was dealt with quite severely by the teacher. Private evaluations (away from the teacher) were, however, much more likely to be of a negative or sarcastic nature: the girls of school C said that boys were very quick to put them down if they made spoken contributions in the classroom.

Evaluation of text was particularly important in English. Pupils especially had to use strategies to evaluate characters in narrative. Evaluation of characters was often compared to the degree to which the author's characterization had aided visualization. This is clearly related to the pupils' understanding of 'language' and narrative structures, and the meta-language, which pupils can use to enable them to carry out the evaluation. Pupils and teachers said that poor understanding of vocabulary often impeded 'evaluation' of texts. Self-support often therefore involved pupils using strategies to resolve their confusion as to the meaning of words. Knowledge of teacher expectations and the criteria by which they value performance and text underpinned the pupils' own evaluation. This was often a difficult factor for pupils as the success criteria for a lesson were often set implicitly. More than once pupils would listen to a lengthy explanation of what was expected of them in a lesson, and the first thing they would ask peers was 'What exactly were they expected to do?'. Targets were often vague.

Gender differences have already been highlighted in respect of boys' propensity to be negative and sarcastic. At least this was the perception of some girls. On the other hand, boys would sometimes make negative and sarcastic comments, not as an evaluation of the work, but more as a jocular remark intended to generate humour. This may have been the function of the comment made by the boys in respect of the girls' performance. In fact, evaluative comments made by boys may be a particular way of boys developing and asserting their gender over girls: humour was seen as important for both boys and girls.

Funny boys were seen to be most popular among boys and girls, except when the humour was used to denigrate others, in which case, this merely generated animosity within the peer group.

Overtly psychological theories that do not account for social and emotional functions of pupil contributions in class clearly miss an important aspect of the life of the classroom.

'Clarification' self-support learning strategies

The 'clarification' cluster of strategies represents an intuitively self-evident cluster. What do pupils do if they do not know what to do in the classroom? This group is almost entirely focused on strategies for establishing procedural aspects of the classroom activity:

- What is the task?
- How will the task be carried out?
- How long have the learners to carry out the task?
- Who will carry out the different parts of the task?

Across all four schools the principal means for clarifying the task was 'questioning'. An example of this can be seen in an interview with a pupil in school D: 'I'd either ask a friend to see what they're doing, to see if I could get some ideas, or, probably ask the teacher again, just to explain it, to go over it.' The pupil explained the sequence in her own mind of the strategy for clarifying work, first, to ask fellow pupils, second, to ask the teacher. Though she talked about asking the teacher, she explained that clarification via a pupil involves 'seeing what they're doing'. Clarification of classroom learning could involve pupils looking at others' work. They ask a peer or they ask the teacher. This was very much the reality of the classroom inter-actions between pupils and teacher. The following questions in a lesson observation were posed by pupils in respect of a newspaper article they were writing:

Pupil 1: So what's actually happening?
Pupil 2: Did he kill Ginger?
Pupil 1: We want something better to grab people's attention. Do we need a picture?
Pupil 2: When do we have to do it by?
Pupil 1: Are we having a full size picture?
Pupil 2: What shall we call it?
Pupil 2: What shall we call it?

There is evidence from this transcription of the use of questioning by pupils to clarify details of the task beyond content. For example, pupils ask each other about the nature of the task ('so what's actually happening?'), time limits ('when do we have to do it by?') and text ('so are we going to do it generally at first?'). The pupils are supporting their own learning by a process of clarifica-tion. To this extent the 'clarification' cluster includes self-support learning strategies. Clarification, in this instance, is by means of open ('what', 'when') and closed ('are we', 'has it') questions directed to each other. So, for instance, in this extract, the pupils discuss:

- the general nature of the task ('nature of the task'): this functions like the collecting together of thoughts prior to commencing the task;
- the manner and format with which the report text is to be written ('text structure'): in this case, the pupil wondered whether a photo was needed for the newspaper report;
- the deadline by which the task must be completed ('task timing').

'Clarification' worked on many more levels. For instance, teachers would give spoken advice about the task, noise levels, ground rules for behaviour and the way they should work with others. Emotional support was sought by pupils and offered by teachers to help pupils understand why they were doing an activity. The proximity to the Year 9 SATs and the move to Year 10, were given as the primary motivations. Pupils were also able to seek clarification from instructions and information recorded at the start of the lesson on the board, or on worksheets. When asked how often they sought clarification from the teacher, pupils in school C said that they rarely had to do so as their teacher almost always gave sufficient support beforehand. Pupils in school B said that they often referred to a display set up by the teacher on the wall, in respect of strategies for proofreading written work. Likewise, the teacher in school C sought to clarify the nature of the texts expected of her pupils, by referring them to some previously produced work, by an older class, which she had displayed on the wall in the classroom.

Reflection

Consider questions raised by pupils in your class. Do you recognize the different functions of questions highlighted above?

Make some notes of the questions asked by your pupils in a lesson. Can you see a range of purposes behind the questions?

- Pupils' initial clarification of a task.
- Pupils seeking feedback on an approach to problem-solving.
- Pupils looking for attention or praise.
- Pupils trying to avoid work.

Strategies for the classroom

'Question time' and 'graffiti boards' for extended writing in KS2 and KS3

Make time for the different types of questions which children ask or want to ask. Rather than holding plenaries at the end of a lesson, plan for explicit progress points during a lesson or a sequence of lessons in which you will ask children for questions to clarify aspects of the work. This could, for instance, include questions about how to phrase a particular idea, choosing between alternatives or sequencing ideas in a text.

Give quieter children a Q-card beforehand to remind them to think of a question for your question time. Question time could be in pairs, groups or as a whole class. It might focus on a key theme in writing or be more responsive to individual queries.

A 'graffiti board' can be set up as part of a display for children to make comments about what they like in other people's writing. This encourages a positive but critically appreciative attitude in young writers.

There may be other reasons behind requests for clarification. The important point here is that professionals in class must understand the different purposes behind pupil questions.

Clarification can exist at a spoken, written or display level. Clarification is predicated on an understanding of the rules for asking questions in whole class and group or paired work: related to the knowledge and understanding of teaching strategies. Pupils have to understand the pedagogical methods used by teachers. For instance, pupils often seek clarification in a slot after the overview explanation given by teachers at the start of the lesson. Their questions may be asked in the whole class setting or where they feel more inhibited by the peer group, they will ask the question when the teacher circulates around the room. Pupils in one school often ask others within their immediate group, then other groups, before they ask the teacher. Pupils confirmed that the most frequent topic for clarification was the meaning or spelling of a word. Pupils from school C said that they often asked for help in phrasing their sentences. The perceptions of the pupils were that the most effective form of clarification by a teacher was not to give the answer 'on a plate'. Teachers often gave learners strategies for solving the problem: resources or techniques for dealing with a particular issue. They would give alternatives to the children and the children would then choose between them. Clarification by the teacher would sometimes enable the children to prioritize aspects of a task, over other parts.

Gender was not seen to be a significant factor in the forms of clarification strategies used by pupils. However, a teacher made an important point about the purposes of pupil questions. A teacher at school C said that in some cases, a request for clarification by pupils would have an ulterior motive. In fact, a pupil might be asking a question to set the teacher up for ridicule, in front of the rest of the class. Interestingly, Edwards and Mercer (1987) highlight the fact that teachers generally ask questions, and pupils respond knowing that the teacher already knows the answer. The point made by the teacher in school C is that when this process is reversed, this can be particularly uncomfortable for the teacher. Pupils here are attempting to gain popularity from their peers by showing up the teacher. This is not here classed as an example of 'clarification'. It is, however, an example of the sort of deviant coping strategy predicted by Pollard (1985), as a response to the competing demands of the school and peer group. On a more positive note, pupils in school B showed in lessons, and explained in interviews, that effective learners sometimes asked clarifying questions to reassure themselves that they were completing the task appropriately. They also saw this as an opportunity to engineer praise from the teacher, rather than waiting for the teacher to come to them, they would go to the teacher to show them how well they were doing. This is not an example of clarification, but it is an example of an affective self-support strategy.

The framework includes a number of clusters of self-support learning strategies, each of which operate within a given context. As previously explained, the analysis of self-support learning strategies is based on classroom observations and interviews with pupils and teachers. In this book a central concern is to capture the reality of learning in schools. The perspectives of pupils are particularly important. Views of learning commonly held by teachers are not always reflected in the views of learners: 'Students conceived of learning as surface level mastery of information and facts, while secondary teachers agreed more strongly with a deep view of learning' (Brown, reported in Kane and Maw 2005: 312). Though the above research by Gavin Brown takes place in New Zealand, the differences in learners' and teachers' perceptions of learning will probably not surprise anyone who works in schools.

Strategies for the classroom

Planning for learning

The following principles will be helpful in developing more engaged learners and less superficial approaches to learning in class.

- Plan activities with children based on areas which they are interested in. Giving ownership of learning to the children will encourage greater independence and motivation.
- Aim for 'pacey' learning over 'pacey' teaching. Remember that the focus should always be on learning.
- While effective teaching is important, this does not mean 'putting on a virtuoso performance' to the detriment of the learner.
- Stay positive in your use of language. Have high expectations of behaviour, quality of work and the work ethic of the class.
- Look for positive learning outcomes. What positive benefits will new knowledge or skills bring the learners?
- Encourage reference to positive role models in the class, school and wider community.
- Learners need time, space and the tools to learn. This means focusing on less content over a longer period of time. Lots of incomplete superficial work is discouraging for both learners and teachers.
- Talk and dialogue for learning are one of the single most essential elements for successful learning. Plan for talk systematically throughout the lesson/ sequence of lessons.
- Involve children in the assessment or their own and each other's learning.

Reflection

Consider your own classes. Would your pupils agree with the above statement about learning made by secondary pupils in New Zealand?

- Why might pupils see learning as a fairly superficial internalization of information presented by teachers?
- How might the activities set up by teachers encourage this approach to learning?

Pupil perspectives on learning

In my interviews with learners in Year 9 English classes, there appeared to be a greater understanding of the strategies used by effective learners in class than is suggested by the research of Brown above. Pupils did not always have sophisticated ways to explain these approaches to learning, but they were eager to discuss them nonetheless. A number of these features are explained and summarized below.

- *The independent learner*: At the outset of my research, 'independent learning' was an important underpinning notion. There was, however, a dichotomy in pupils' thinking. On the one hand, some suggested that an independent learner worked on their own, with no support from their peers. The aim of independent learning according to a teacher in school D was for learners to prepare effectively for successful GCSE exams. Another strand of thought recognized that the truly independent learner is able to draw on social resources in the peer group, rather than working in isolation. It seemed to be a feature of the interviews with all pupils that they had not considered the importance of working with others as a part of independent learning. Indeed, when they started to consider that getting on with the peer group as well as getting on with the work were both important, their views changed. My own view changed in respect of this concept. While independent learning was seen to be the ideal, the position has moved towards an analysis of learning in a network of interdependencies, within which pupils operate in school (see Chapter 3).
- *Praise management*: Though one might think that effective learners are likely to be confident, pupils reported that this was not always the case. However, they did recognize that effective learners have strategies to support their own self-esteem and motivation. They suggested that effective learners are able to manufacture opportunities within

their learning to receive praise from their teacher. An example from one school suggests that pupils asked questions of their teacher in the full knowledge that they were making good progress in writing a newspaper report, and that the teacher was going to tell them this publicly. This can happen during the performance of an activity. Clarification is sometimes sought from the teacher, with the full knowledge that the learners are likely to receive very positive feedback from the teacher. This also happens at the end of the lesson when pupils would show the teacher their completed work. 'Praise management' works at two levels. Not only does it enable learners to reinforce their self-esteem and hence maintain motivation, it also works on a social level to develop the relationship with the teacher. The teacher is therefore likely to have a continuingly positive image of the pupil.

- *Writing in 'series' vs writing in 'parallel'*: Many pupils write collaborative projects in pairs or in larger groups of four or five. Writing individual parts of a text often happen in isolation and it is only towards the point of completion that the different pieces of writing are joined together. In essence, none of the writing observed was of a truly collaborative nature in Hewitt (2004). Fieldnotes written up at the time of observation speculated that two forms of group or paired-writing were existed. One commonly observed strategy involved individuals writing in 'series' different parts of the text. Individuals or sub-groups within a larger group worked on parts of a text and then simply joined the parts together when the work came to completion. In this approach, cohesion within the newly-created text was rarely considered. In such texts, therefore, the group writing could appear a little disjointed.

  Another logical option, not observed in this research, would involve pupils working collaboratively in 'parallel', jointly contributing to and developing a text together. One example close to this in school B actually involved one pupil dictating to another. Although the free-flow of ideas between learners did not take place as might have been anticipated, the pupils did discuss the choice of ideas and words as they created the new text. Pupils said that they would always generally write in 'series'; however, as a variation, they may adopt the transcriber/composer approach, especially where one person was seen to have neater handwriting compared to another. Depressingly, this latter approach was often the organization employed in larger groups, where some of the members would sit back and let others complete the work for them.

- *Creativity through dialogue*: Pupil strategies for developing creative ideas in discussion were very interesting. Though some boys wanted to get straight on to the activity rather than prepare for it in some form of discussion, more effective learners tend to talk it through. Pupils' suggestions are discussed, agreed, disagreed, modified, extended and elaborated upon. This is often accompanied by humour from both boys and girls, and by sarcasm from boys. The decision as to the choice of competing ideas is not always made on the basis of quality. Strategies for decision-making range from the sympathetic ('encouraging quieter pupils to contribute'), to the emotional ('shouting the loudest') to the democratic ('by an informal vote').

Boys' and girls' perspectives on learning

Discussions with pupils and teachers generated some important interpretations of the use of self-support learning strategies by boys and girls. The differences centred on organization for learning, preparation for learning, confidence and choice of reading matter:

- *Organization*: According to teachers and pupils in Hewitt (2004), girls tend to choose friends of similar academic abilities, whereas boys tend to choose friends of differing academic abilities. Therefore, when given a choice of who they can sit and work with (groupings were predominantly based on friendship), girls would sit with 'like' ability, and boys with differing abilities. Furthermore, it was suggested that girls prefer to work in smaller groups (pairs or threes), whereas boys prefer to work in larger groups (fours or above). One very large group of ten boys worked quite effectively. But for planning purposes, they worked in smaller sub-groups of about three, where a smaller forum was better. Given the choice to work in mixed or single-sex classes, most pupils would choose to work in mixed-sex classes. Not, however, for academic reasons, but according to the pupils because they 'have more of a laugh'. In fact, there was some debate among girls in a single-sex class as to whether single-sex lessons favour girls, but not boys; whereas they said that mixed-sex classes were seen to favour neither, at an academic level. They felt boys tended to be more gregarious in their work. Humour, sarcasm and imitation are all strategies for use in the lesson.
- *Preparation for learning*: Boys were seen to want to get straight on to an activity, whereas girls were more likely to discuss and plan their work before starting it. Thus where writing frames are used in English to encourage planning for writing, this can be seen as something of an encumbrance for boys. One group of pupils said, 'Boys write, then discuss, girls discuss, then write.' It must be remembered that these judgements are based on a specific corpus of data, and there is no

evidence that the claims generalize for all boys and girls; however, it is interesting in its own right that this was the perception of the participants interviewed for this research.

- *Confidence*: Even very able boys and girls were equally low in confidence about a range of aspects in English, especially writing (including handwriting and spelling). The general view, however, was that boys were less confident than girls in the subject. This could be due to a range of factors, such as the boys' perception that girls were more able in English, had better handwriting, and or even that it was not 'cool' for boys to do well in English, or indeed to make spoken contributions in front of a whole class. Some individuals (usually boys) adopt roles within the group to give themselves confidence and to promote themselves and their popularity. This is often a coping strategy for the boys. Likewise, humour is an important affective self-help for boys to secure promotion within the peer group, including girls, and it is a way of maintaining their motivation for otherwise unpalatable activities.
- *Choice of reading materials*: Boys are not always interested in the books which teachers offer as set texts. In some cases they are seen as 'uncool', and therefore uninteresting. An example of this was *Tom's Midnight Garden*, which some boys thought was not very interesting. However, when told about this the teacher responded by obtaining a copy of *The Machine Gunners*, which the boys in one school said was much more motivating. There is no clear-cut evidence from this research as to what books boys and girls read outside of school. Interestingly, one girl said that she would read the books that her mother was reading at any one time.

The significance of the above points must be tempered, given the small number of interviewees in the underpinning research of Hewitt (2004); however, the validity of these statements rests on the fact that for these pupils in these schools, this is the way that they see learning, these are the strategies they use, and these are their perceptions about boys and girls in the classroom.

Self-support strategies and self-regulation

In the past two decades, terminology and the associated conceptual framework have developed from learning strategies (Nisbet and Shucksmith 1986), through to self-regulated learning (Bokaerts 2000). Where do self-support learning strategies fit into this framework?

It is important that self-support strategies are not equated with the strategies of self-regulation: the form may be similar, but the function is very different. Thus, Zimmerman (2000) proposes a model of self-regulation, which includes three phases in the completion of a task: forethought, performance and self-reflection. Where someone is merely enacting a task or activity which is within their capacity, the process of self-regulation supports the completion of the task. However, where a teacher expects the learner to work at a level above their capacity, then the strategies function differently to support the learner successfully to achieve something which they could not previously achieve. This is a qualitative difference, but one which explains why self-support strategies are important tools for the learner to support their own journey through the 'zone of proximal development' (Vygotsky 1978) even though they may be being led by the teacher at that time.

An alternative approach to this conceptual issue is to recognize that all learning is constructed within a social setting. The more able and effective learners will be able to implement strategies of self-supported learning to enable them to make progress in their learning: at the level of cognitive, affective, social and moral development. Weinstein et al. (2000) suggest that many learners get stuck at the level of understanding what they have to do in a learning task (a problem of 'meta-comprehension'). This was observed in learners in each of the schools for the research in Hewitt (2004). For example, in developing the plan for a soap opera in school A, some pupils did not know how to represent the characters and settings, so they asked the teacher. In school B, pupils did not know which character they were expected to write a newspaper report about, so they asked another group. In school C, pupils were successful in planning a joint piece of narrative description, but struggled to avoid using the same adjectives, so they used a thesaurus to help them develop alternative vocabulary. In school D, a negative evaluation of a role-play performance was improved by a pair of girls appealing for alternative evaluations by other members of the class.

The important point here is that pupils use a range of strategies to support their learning at different points in a lesson including when they experience difficulties. The strategies help pupils to continue in their learning. If these strategies are not available, then the likelihood is that learning activities will not continue and the potential for effective learning in each area will be reduced.

Summary of implications for the teacher

Know the self-support learning strategies which are used and not used by their pupils

- Every classroom, every school and every phase of education is likely to have a distinctive profile of self-support strategies present in the classroom.

Encourage dialogue on all learning activities

- Pupils' suggestions are discussed, agreed, disagreed, modified, extended and elaborated upon. These are the benefits of pupils working together.

Ensure that collaborative writing makes sense

- Where pupils work separately in pairs or as a group on a project, cohesion in the newly-created text is rarely considered. Does it fit together? Does it flow?

Humour works on different levels

- It helps pupils and their teacher get through the lesson.
- It helps boys establish themselves in their peer group.
- It provides a link to popular culture.
- It can be sarcastic and used as a 'put-down', especially by boys.

Be very clear about the work required of pupils

- For some pupils, completing a task means filling the available paper, filling the available time or indeed accomplishing a particular type of text according to the demands of the teacher.

Encourage leadership in their pupils

- Some pupils see themselves as leaders.
- The leadership role can change hands throughout a lesson according to the demands of the task.

Make sure that pupils have access to classroom reference materials and useful resources

- Having dictionaries, thesauruses and other reference material available for pupils to access encourages a self-regulatory approach to learning.

Clarify the meaning of technical or difficult vocabulary

- Pupils say that this is the main reason for not understanding a task or an activity.

Offer opportunities throughout a lesson for pupils to clarify their work

- Learners cannot always express confusion over an activity.
- Remember that most questions are asked to confirm an interpretation already made by a learner.
- Pupils ask questions to gain confidence and praise for their work.
- Questions can be asked as a deviant strategy for putting the teacher 'on the spot' and to make them feel uncomfortable.

Tasks involve evaluation at different levels

- Reflection on features of learning and behaviour: text, own/peer performance and task (teacher expectations, content, quantity, quality, method and performance against targets).

5 Learning strategies and the teacher

> Teachers today are more likely to develop their understanding about teaching despite the conditions in which they work rather than because of them.
>
> (Hatch et al. 2005: 323)

This chapter will help you to:

- identify the role of the teacher in developing learning strategies;
- understand the principles of contingent teaching.

The above are words of teacher educators in the United States. Few could say that the British government has not invested heavily in teacher development and the development of professional networks. One such example is the network of schools associated with the Primary National Strategy (DfES 2003). However, not all teachers have benefited from the opportunities afforded by the Primary National Strategy networks and Continuing Professional Development opportunities. For this reason, I would like to explore some of the issues around teaching and the development of effective learning. The role of the teacher in supporting and developing learning is a complex and subtle one.

Teachers and learners

Teachers use a variety of strategies to coax children into a positive and fruitful experience of learning. After all, children of different ages can and do enjoy learning in school. It could be that they value the principle of learning new information in a particular area of learning (a judgement on moral grounds). It could be that they are motivated to do so because if they do not, then they will face disciplinary measures (a judgement on affective grounds). It could be that they want to do the activity because their friends want to do so (a judgement on social grounds), or indeed they might want to learn new skills to become more able in that subject (a judgement on cognitive grounds).

Reflection

Make a list of the activities which your pupils find interesting and/or motivating. Make a list of activities where you have had to work hard as a teacher to get the children to complete the work.
Can you explain the differences in these activities?
What factors are at play?

- the topic;
- the way you teach;
- the way pupils perceive the importance of the work?

Strategies for the classroom

'Past, present and future': end-of-year evaluations

Pupils often find the process of evaluating their learning to be tedious and pointless. You could make this more engaging with the following activity:

1 Take a piece of paper in landscape form.
2 Fold it in three so that you have three columns down the page.
3 At the top of the columns write 'past', 'present', 'future', respectively.
4 Ask the children to reflect on what they have enjoyed learning and what they have learned at different points of their school lives.
5 'Past' learning might be thinking about previous years.
6 'Present' learning could be this year.
7 'Future' learning could be a consideration of priorities for next year.

This activity can provide a great insight into a learner's own view of their progress, what they enjoy doing in school and their motivation for learning.

In Chapter 4, we heard pupils' views of what motivated them in the class. The ability to identify goals to motivate yourself at the short- and long-term levels is identified as an important learning strategy by Zimmerman (2000). One could argue that the longer-term goal of a good job is less the result of a learning strategy, and more subject to the influence of the parents and the peer culture.

When asked about structure and behaviour management in relation to more challenging children, pupils discussed motivation:

Pupil: Yeah, there's a couple. There's some in every class.

Researcher:	Why do you think that is the case then?
Pupil:	I think it's because they think it's cool. But then in later life they're gonna be the one's who pay for it 'cos they won't end up with a very good job.
Researcher:	So from the people in your group, C—, M— learning, and being independent and learning successfully, is that seen to be cool or uncool?
Pupil:	It depends what lesson it is and what piece of work you're doing, people at the moment like learning because it's real life and people enjoy doing it. But if it's about books that people think are a bit sad then they won't enjoy doing it.

Pupils and teachers had different views on what motivated them. Several of the teachers saw SATs, preparation for Year 10 and ultimately success in the GCSE exams as important 'motivators' for the Year 9 pupils. For example, a teacher in one school explains in a lesson why she feels that writing a report about the novel *Stone Cold* (Swindells 1995) will help pupils to prepare for the following Year 10:

> There's an awful lot. What I've tried to do, everything to help you out. I've tried to go through all the skills you'll be using next year. Each of those skills you will be using. Audience form and layout. You're trying to persuade people. Your audience. It will be very important next year for your work. This is the last piece of work before next year. Hopefully it will give you an idea about the kind of work that you'll be doing in Y10.
>
> (Lesson observed in Year 9)

Teachers support learners in specific activities ('audience form and layout' for writing in English), but relate it to the longer term as pupils approach key transition points. I suspect that the longer-term perspective is more important for older children rather than younger children. It is interesting therefore that the classic conception of the zone of proximal development sees the teacher supporting the learner in the early stages of learning new skills or performing a new activity. As the latter becomes more able to take on responsibility for the action, control will be handed over to the latter. The learner will at some point take full control, regulating their own performance. According to Wood (1998), in the early years, this may involve supporting important functions such as helping the learner to pay attention, concentrate or recall items from memory. Conscious understanding of the ability is only the final product of the development of self-regulation (Wertsch and Addison-Stone 1985).

If this conceptual framework is translated to the classroom, how can it account for the processes of learning? The zone of proximal development can account for this situation, but it will require a reinterpretation of the role of the learner and the teacher.

What do pupils bring to the learning process? How can teachers respond to this? In English, of all subjects, these are particularly important questions, since pupils are required to demonstrate knowledge and understanding of texts and issues which are open to interpretation. Opinions must be justified with evidence, and arguments must be well founded with a logical sequence of thought. Their interpretations of and responses to texts, though mediated by the pedagogical support of the teacher, will nevertheless be further mediated by the prior knowledge, attitudes and skills, which the learners bring to the activity.

The traditional conception of the passage through the 'zone of proximal development', is of a teacher leading a learner by the hand down an avenue, and at a certain point when they are able to find their own way to the destination, the teacher lets go and the pupil makes their way until they reach the end of the road. The pupil comes on the journey, sometimes with an idea of how to get to the destination, maybe with a compass, a map or the ability to ask passing people the right direction. The pupil may be a willing traveller. They may like and respect the person they are travelling with, or indeed they may be so scared of that person that they are only travelling under coercion. Their intention may be to shoot off down a side alley, as soon as the opportunity arises! Others may accompany the child on the journey, happy to enjoy the social interaction.

Alternatively, as the teacher and pupil walk down this road of learning, there may be a gang of kids jeering mockingly at the pupil. For some pupils this may be enough to deter them on their journey, others may be resilient enough to ignore such distractions, and others may have to weigh up the choice between popularity within the peer group, and a successful trip along the road to learning. Of course, this metaphor can be taken further – what if the local community is hostile to those who walk the road of learning?

Pupils bring skills, knowledge and attitudes, which can facilitate or indeed block their passage through the zone of proximal development. This is the pupils' learning journey (Figure 5.1).

Paris (1988) warns of the danger of overextending a metaphor for learning, beyond the available evidence. This metaphor does, however, explain that the learner is active and they are not passive recipients of new skills or knowledge. Nor are they like clay, moulded by the teacher, until the correct form is achieved, at which point the shape is retained exactly as required. Cognitive, as well as affective, social and moral factors will influence the learners passing through the zone of proximal development. Demetriou (2000) explains that temperament, personality and cognition are so intertwined that affective states will impact on learning dispositions (teachers will relate closely to this notion).

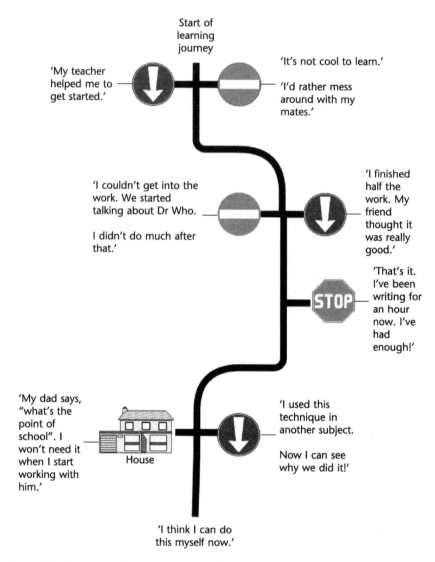

Figure 5.1 Support and barriers on a 'learning journey'

Pupils bring to the learning journey learning strategies, knowledge and contextual understandings which can support, have no effect or indeed hinder the learner. Among these are self-support learning strategies and the knowledge and understanding which underpin them.

While the teacher lends support for an activity, the effective learner will adopt self-support strategies to facilitate their passage through the zone of proximal development. By lending positive support to the instructional input, or where the teacher's input is not appropriate, self-support strategies are used to feed back to the teacher in order to ensure a more appropriate form of instructional input. Learners can alert their teachers if they do not understand part of an activity. This presents the teacher with an opportunity to resolve the misunderstanding. Of course the teacher may or may not decide to take this opportunity. In that situation, the learner is helping the teacher to fine-tune their teaching to a level that the pupil perceives is right for them.

Dweck (1999) along with Zimmerman (2000) highlight the phenomena of 'learned helplessness', where pupils become overly dependent on others to complete any learning activity; and 'perceived self-efficacy', the learner's own perception of their learner potential. Thus, a pupil who overly uses support strategies to clarify features of an activity may be masking a low perception of their own learning potential, even where their actual learning potential is much higher. They may be seeking support when they really do not need it. Zimmerman (2000) would consider that they have low perceptions of their own self-efficacy. Dweck (1999) would say that the learner is in danger of becoming over-dependent on support from others. The apparent paradox here is that self-support strategies can lead to over-dependence on other people in class.

Contingent teaching

The relationship between teaching strategies and pupil self-support learning strategies is a dynamic one. Wood (1988) proposed a 'principle of contingency' by which teachers help children to construct local expertise (connected with that particular task or group of tasks) by focusing their attention on relevant and timely aspects of the task, and by highlighting things they need to take account of. This principle also encourages teachers to break the task down into a sequence of smaller tasks that children can manage to perform. Wood suggests that effective teaching through the zone of proximal development gives only that level of support which enables the learner to accomplish it successfully: combining a suitable level of challenge and support. Wood states, however, that, in the real world of the classroom, achieving contingent instruction is far more difficult than is suggested by the largely 'experimental' evidence of constructive activities between adults and one or two children. Wood considers that many lessons taught in school often involve tasks that do not have a clear, obvious structure and may not yield single 'right answers'. As Pollard (1985) would say, this reflects the dilemma that pupils and teachers face in the classroom, leading to the development of coping strategies, in order to balance the competing and often irreconcilable issues.

Reflection

Make a note of the forms of support which you offer learners in one of your classes:

- How do you know when children need support in their learning?
- How much support do you offer?
- What form of support for learning do you offer?
- How does this support help the learning maintain independence?
- If not, do you find that some pupils have a tendency to be over-reliant on your support?

Strategies for the classroom

Learning support plans

While Individual Education Plans (IEPs) are commonly used to set targets and plans of support for children with Special Educational Needs, all children should consider the types of support available to them. This is a feature of 'personalized' learning. Each plan could consider the following:

- the child's view of their learning;
- areas where they feel they need more support;
- simple and child-friendly targets for the medium and short term;
- a record of significant achievements.

Previous attempts at recording achievement have often been too ambitious, trying to do too much, very much distant from the learner. Many teachers may remember the Record of Achievements introduced into schools in the early 1990s only to be abandoned soon after as being unworkable.

Pupils may or may not have previous experiences of using the strategies. The learning process is a dynamic one, characterized by an interplay of teaching and pupil learning strategies. Effective learning involves the optimum interaction of teaching strategies and pupil self-support learning strategies. Passage through the zone of development is *socially constructed* and is an *affective construct*: a reconciliation of competing interests (as in Pollard's model of coping strategies). Self-support strategies have been situated within the social constructivist frameworks of Vygotsky (1978), the sociological framework of Pollard (1985), and the socio-cognitive principles of Dweck (1999) and Demetriou (2000).

Nisbet and Shucksmith (1986) highlight conceptions of classroom instruction in English primary classrooms of the 1980s. There have been many studies of various categories of teachers based on classroom observations. Galton (1989) in the seminal work of the ORACLE project identified a range of approaches to teaching based on the degree of interaction, organization of the classroom and learning resources. These were illustrated as various 'types' of teachers: group monitors, class inquirers, infrequent changers, individual monitors, habitual changers and rotating changers. It comes as no surprise that some of the important characteristics of effective teaching closely match the profile of learning strategies highlighted by Nisbet and Shucksmith earlier. Schallert and Kleiman (1979) listed the following important features:

- tailoring the message to the learner's existing level of understanding;
- reminding the learner of linked ideas and topics, already encountered;
- focusing attention on relevant facts;
- monitoring understanding through questioning and evaluation, while encouraging the learner to utilize these approaches themselves.

Brown and Campione (1977) highlight the effectiveness of the teacher modelling learning strategies, which the learner is encouraged to use with support at first, but with the expectation that they will gradually take control of the task as they become more adept. The internalization of the so-called 'Socratic dialogue' in effect not only helps the learner to use self-questioning, but ultimately also results in greater understanding of current and future activities and problems.

The concept of 'contingent teaching' can be extended to cover all strategies used by both teacher and pupils to regulate the levels of support for learning. For instance, effective teaching and learning require the use of an appropriate level of learning strategies to ensure that pupils are making the most effective progress: a balance of challenge and support. From the point of view of the learner, the principle of contingency requires that they use self-support strategies (Figure 5.2).

Self-support strategies and the teacher

The clusters of self-support strategies appear to fall within different phases of a lesson. These mirror the forethought, performance and self-reflection phases posited by Zimmerman (2000). Logically the strategies could be used in any one of the phases, in specific phases only or in more than one of the phases. I would like to suggest this as a possible model of learning. Figure 5.3 gives an overview of the proposed sequence of self-support learning strategies.

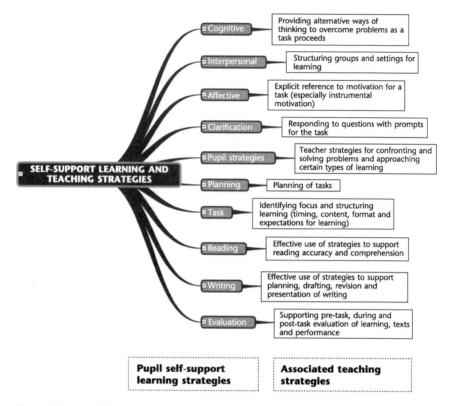

Figure 5.2 Pupil self-support learning strategies and associated teaching strategies

---

Reflection

Find time to focus on one sequence of learning. It might go over several days or even several weeks according to the topic. You could keep an informal diary of the following:

• Note the various strategies (see above) which a group of able children use to successfully complete the work.

• Are certain strategies used at different points in the learning journey by pupils?

• Compare this to the strategies which a group of less able learners use. What is the difference?

• What could you do to encourage, model or develop the use of self-support strategies in your pupils?

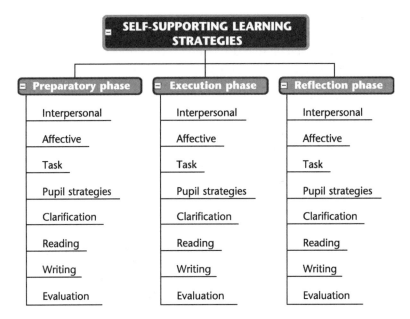

Figure 5.3   Phases in the use of self-support learning strategies

---

Strategies for the classroom

Learning films

Teachers often watch films of classroom activities for the purposes of professional development. But how often do children look at their own learning on film?

- In one example, a Year 9 class prepared news reports of different types which were then recorded on film.
- Pupils were asked to evaluate the work according to set criteria.
- The films were watched several times over by the children, analysing what was good and what was not so good.

It's important to set ground rules for the analysis and evaluation. Actually pupils were quite protective of others following overly negative comments.

It might be expected in any one lesson that the sequence shown in Figure 5.3 would be present, with a selection of the strategies being used in the three phases of preparation, execution and reflection. Virtually all clusters of self-support learning strategies are present throughout the sequence of a lesson. Why is this the case? The tasks required of pupils at each of the schools obliged them to carry out an activity over a sequence of lessons.

- In school A, pupils planned an original soap opera.
- In school B, pupils read from the novel *Stone Cold* (Swindells 1995) and then on the basis of one of the principal characters wrote a newspaper report telling the story from their point of view.
- In school C, pupils completed their own ending to a piece of narrative description.
- In school D, pupils researched the case of Derek Bentley, and then produced a *News at Ten*-style news report role-play. This last example will illustrate that self-support strategy clusters can appear at any point in the sequence of the unit of work.

There is a tendency for certain self-support strategy clusters to appear during the three phases of the unit of work. For example, in school D, comparison of the sequence of self-support strategy clusters reveals that the 'task', 'evaluation', 'clarification', 'interpersonal' and 'affective' clusters are present in the early stages of the unit of work. A long introduction by the teacher about a unit of work on the Derek Bentley case clarified how she wanted pupils to prepare and deliver a role-play performance to illustrate the principal issues of the case. This was linked to an evaluation of the pupils' progress against National Curriculum (QCA 1999) descriptors. In setting targets for the pupils in terms of her expectations, the teacher also explained the purposes of the activity to support pupil motivation. Performance of the task took place over three lessons, during which pupils employed 'interpersonal', 'clarification', 'planning', 'task', 'pupil strategies', 'reading' and 'writing'.

It was confusing to see 'evaluation' strategies from the initial stages of the unit, through to the reflection and concluding phases of the work. When the use of self-support learning strategies is seen in context, this seems to be less odd. First, lessons started with an evaluation by the pupils, following prompting by the teacher, of where they were following on from the most recent work. Second, most lessons finished with a short informal plenary by the teacher, in which the teacher asked the pupils again to reflect on and evaluate the success of the lesson. To explain the use of 'evaluation' strategies throughout the lesson, it is necessary to analyse the role of the teacher while the pupils are working in their groups on completing the task. The teacher, following an oft used approach, circulates around the classroom, visiting each of the pairs or groups to offer support and most interestingly to ask them questions, in order to provoke an evaluation by the learner of the progress they have made up to that point in the lesson. The 'progress evaluation' helped the pupils to recognize the progress they have made towards meeting the expectations for the lesson and the unit of work, as well as offering some opportunities to focus the learners' attention on important or neglected aspects of the task. Observation of the lessons in school D confirmed the spread of self-support strategies throughout the unit of work.

Any evaluation of the proposed sequence of self-support strategy clusters might argue that compared to models such as that of Zimmerman (2000), the picture seems to be less straightforward than is suggested elsewhere. That is because an analysis of the reality of the classroom reveals that the pattern of strategy use is far too complex over a unit of work to justifiably posit a black and white picture of strategy use. Lessons are so very different in themselves, and it is understandable that according to the point a class has reached in a sequence of work, almost any one of the self-support learning strategies may be present. Based on the data obtained for this research 'reading' and 'writing' self-support strategies were not seen at the end of a unit of work, because presumably at this point the tasks had been completed and there was no longer any need to use such strategies. Though, of course, it is conceivable that in evaluating a piece of written work, pupils might be involved in both reading and writing.

Teacher and pupil perspectives

The classic process in social constructivist models of instruction involves the modelling and demonstration of activities by teachers, prior to guided and then independent performance by the learner (Wood 1998). As has been explained above, those strategies demonstrated by the teacher, at an inter-psychological level should then be internalized by the learner. It would be expected therefore that if the teacher promoted a strategy for self-supported learning, then there should be some evidence of the use of such measures by pupils. Of course, that is not always the case; and that was one of the findings of this research. Teachers often believe that the strategies that they promote are actually used by learners, and have a positive impact in the classroom. That is not a criticism of the teachers; it is merely the reality of the classroom. The results of the research are summarized as follows:

- *Literacy and thinking skills programmes*: One example of this is in the teaching of literacy and thinking skills programmes as distinct, but rather decontextualized, programmes. There were two examples of this emanating from my research: separate literacy lessons as part of the Key Stage 3 English Strategy; and a short Thinking Skills programme promoted specifically by school C. In both cases, the programmes were very worksheet-based and were seen as such by pupils, despite the efforts of the teachers involved. Apparently, where such lessons do not relate to other aspects of the curriculum, or are seen to be too worksheet-based, then they are summarily dismissed by pupils as being irrelevant: 'Literacy, oh yeah, you mean worksheets. That's boring' (Pupil in school C, 2001). Teachers actually do recognize these problems, but sometimes they are at the mercy of national and local developments, over which they have no control. Literacy was seen by some teachers as being something of a threat to the traditional and much-valued conception of English. The form of literacy which promotes a mechanical overly grammatical approach, is criticized by some teachers. However important this is for teachers at a professional level, it does not seem to have impinged on the consciousness of pupils, who seemed quite oblivious to this debate.

- *Targets*: Schools often work very hard to set targets, and to motivate their pupils to do well in the Year 9 SATs tests. There were detailed targets set by pupils for aspects of English. However, depressingly for many teachers, pupils took little notice of the targets, and the SATs themselves were not seen as being that significant by the children interviewsed in this research. Likewise, exams in their own right were not seen as being significant to pupils, except where they offer gateways to the future. For teachers, exams (SATs or GCSEs) are significant measures of accountability, and therefore mean something different to teachers compared with their pupils. Pupils see the writing up of targets in their planners and exercise books as routines, which have little meaning for them. These might be designated 'performance targets', as opposed to 'learning targets' within the lesson, which are seen by pupils as being an important part of the support that teachers are able to give. This mirrors the distinction made by Dweck (1999) between motivation for 'performance' and 'mastery' learning. She considered 'performance learning' as motivation for surface aspects of learning and meeting externally set judgements of learning effectiveness, while 'mastery learning' relates to motivation focused on learning for its own sake. In the latter conception, motivation for true understanding of a learning task, skill or concept was seen to be more enduring than low level attainment of performance targets divorced from understanding.
- *Planning*: Teachers frequently promote a process approach to writing: it is a significant part of the National Curriculum (QCA 1999). This involves planning, drafting, reviewing, revising, proofreading and presentation. Most teachers promoted planning, drafting and presentation of some kind, but, despite the rhetoric, gave little evidence of achieving the others. Less prominent still was the use of such a process by pupils. Based on the evidence of my research, planning for many pupils is limited to a quick brainstorm diagram, if it is carried out at all. This is quite an issue for teachers and learners, because without sufficient planning, pupils are less likely to be able to show cohesion and coherence in their use of appropriate vocabulary, grammar and structure.

- *Confidence*: One major area in which pupils' and teachers' views diverged considerably was in the 'affective' aspect of learning. Teachers emphasized a lack of pupils' confidence, and sought ways of promoting confidence for all their pupils. Pupils also did see the importance of confidence, but this was not the only affective consideration of pupils. Pupils saw affective considerations as being central to their success in the classroom. Affective self-support strategies could support pupils through to the successful completion of a difficult topic. Affective strategies, such as the use of humour, sarcasm and joking are important measures of success and popularity, especially in boys. Verbal jousting is common among boys. Boys interviewed in my research suggested that this not only dissipates the 'negatives' associated with a particular activity or subject, but it also allows them to score valuable points in the peer group, often at the expense of competitors.

- *Clarification of vocabulary and spelling*: The most commonly occurring problem in English is in relation to vocabulary. Pupils say that they cannot understand the meaning of an unknown word, or they may need help with the spelling of words. Pupils often have an idea as to which meaning or spelling is correct, and their request for clarification is more a seeking of reassurance than a genuine question. Teachers often recognize this latter point. Second, the expressive features of English hold more potential for stress than do others. By this, I mean the production of text in written and especially in spoken form. Speaking in front of a group is seen as being particularly difficult for pupils (especially girls) as they feel exposed in front of the peer group to mockery (especially from boys). Pupils see the role of the teacher as one of supporting and helping children, but not to make it too easy for them. Teachers should help pupils understand what they need to know for the National Curriculum (QCA 1999) and GCSEs.

Logically pupils will use some of the self-support strategies promoted by teachers. However, in reality, few teachers consider the range of strategies which pupils might use to support their own learning.

Objectives-led learning and teaching

Crawford (1999) identified some of the problems associated with a curriculum built on behaviourist principles in the teaching of information technology (IT) in secondary schools:

- Inflexible curricula cannot easily accommodate new and rapidly changing technologies.

- Teachers expect the IT NC to tell them what to teach but it is vague.
- IT teachers are unlikely to be 'gods of knowledge'.
- IT teachers are likely to find traditional didactic teaching strategies much less effective.
- Traditional relationships between pupils and teachers are undermined by the shift from the perception of teachers as 'gods of knowledge' to directors of or leaders in the pursuit of knowledge.
- Active styles of learning in IT can conflict with passive styles of learning prevalent in other school subjects.
- Pupils' questioning of received knowledge is likely to undermine the traditional authoritarian role of the teacher.
- Didactic teaching and individual assessment rarely accommodate collaborative learning.
- Team teaching is more common as IT teachers work with teachers of other subjects, and this reduces the autonomy of individual teachers.
- The separation of content and context prevalent in many other subjects is much less acceptable in IT as it more obviously leads to a sterile learning experience.

(Wilson 1997, quoted in Crawford 1999: 57–8)

The possibilities of technology have in many respects overtaken a restricted curriculum which has been burdened with an objectives-led behaviourist approach. For different reasons, Wilson's analysis of teaching in secondary IT questions an approach in which learning is substantially controlled by the teacher. In place of this, Crawford (1999: 61) proposes a constructivist approach to teaching and learning which does the following:

1 encourages and accepts pupil autonomy;
2 nurtures pupils' curiosity and interest;
3 designs learning environments and experiences rather than selecting instructional strategies leading to particular learning outcomes;
4 sets authentic, open-ended tasks and expects pupils to modify them;
5 describes tasks using a variety of media and presentational perspectives, for example, stories, numbers, rules, statistical summaries, photographs, sound and video;
6 uses real raw data and primary sources, and provides a variety of analytic tools so that pupils can develop their own understandings from different perspectives, that is, accept multiple perspectives;
7 asks pupils to brainstorm, create, invent, question, classify, analyse and predict;
8 asks pupils to elaborate their initial responses;
9 directs pupils towards tasks that might help them identify errors,

confront misconceptions or engender contradictions to their initial hypotheses;

10 always enquires about pupils' understandings, waits for pupils to respond and accepts their responses before sharing generally accepted concepts; that is, emphasizes knowledge construction not reproduction;

11 uses scaffolding to help pupils perform beyond the limits of their ability in the zone of proximal development;

12 encourages dialogue and collaborative learning;

13 encourages the development of cognitive strategies and attitudes as well as memorizing verbal or factual information, motor skills and intellectual skills;

14 assesses processes as well as products;

15 facilitates and guides rather than instructs;

16 keeps an open mind, and accepts that pupils will not always learn what teachers intend.

Constructivism is long established as a theoretical explanation of learning: namely, Piaget, Bruner and Vygotsky (outlined in Wood 1998). This approach underpins many of the professional developments in teaching since the mid-1990s. In primary schools, there has been great emphasis attached to the notion of 'whole-class interactive' teaching for both 'literacy' and 'numeracy'. Debra Myhill (Myhill and Warren 2005) has been at the forefront of those who have questioned the 'interactive' nature of such teaching and whether it does actually enhance learning. While agreeing with Vygotsky that language shapes learning, she goes on to analyse the shortfall in many of the 'critical moments' in classroom learning. She explains in particular that the emphasis on quick-fire questioning with little room for the learner to express their own opinions has reduced the quality of children's learning. Teacher control of discourse in this case is seen to act as a 'strait-jacket' for learning.

In comparison, Wells (1986) recorded parent–child interactions where parents accepted and indeed extended the thinking of their children by deliberately trying to understand them. I do not believe that teachers go out of their way to ignore the views of children or to avoid expanding on their developing ideas. But I recognize that the ability to listen to and build on the ideas of 30 plus children in a class is indeed a challenge. In line with the concept of 'coping strategies', then the so-called interactive approach to teaching is indeed a coping strategy adopted by teachers to deal with a practically impossible context. As Myhill and Warren (2005: 68) say: 'scaffolding [of learning] becomes little more tha a set of prompts, often carefully managed, to elicit a particular response'.

If teachers want to engage children in challenging learning, it is important that the pupils' views and understandings of learning are considered by teachers. This requires time and space in what is a very crowded curriculum and timetable. Pupils must be allowed the time to explore new areas of learning on their own terms. If what Myhill explains is true, then today's classes risk being no more than choreographed exchanges between teachers and pupils, with the teacher firmly in control of the direction of discussion and learning.

That being the case, how is it that many children are successful in school and gain a great deal of pleasure from interesting and thought-provoking classroom activities? Why should children want to place themselves in a position of dependency on others? Pollard's (1985) analysis suggested that the decision to engage with learning goals set by the teacher is not an automatic one. Most teachers will recognize that learners sometimes engage and sometimes they do not. Sometimes pupils passively disengage from the lesson or indeed actively use strategies to obstruct the passage of learning in the classroom. No one would ever suggest that there are simple explanations or solutions to such situations.

Summary of implications for the teacher

Teaching and pupil learning strategies can work together

- While the teacher lends support for an activity, the effective learner will adopt self-support strategies to facilitate their passage through the zone of proximal development.
- By lending positive support to the instructional input, or where the teacher's input is not appropriate, self-support strategies are used to feed back to the teacher in order to ensure a more appropriate form of instructional input.
- Learners can alert their teachers if they do not understand part of an activity.

Effective teaching combines a suitable level of challenge and support

- By offering too much support, the teacher can create a state of learned helplessness.

An effective learner helps the teacher to fine-tune their teaching to a level that the pupil perceives is right for them

- Pupils with a poor view of their effectiveness as a learner may be less inclined to take responsibility for their learning. This can contribute to a state of learned helplessness.

All self-support learning strategies can be present throughout the sequence of a lesson

- Teachers may start a lesson with evaluation and finish a lesson by developing a plan for a future lesson or piece of work.

Do not take for granted the effectiveness of established teaching and learning routines

- Cross-curricular English work is not effective unless it is properly embedded in other work.
- Targets chosen and set by the teacher may be part of the school approach but may not be acted upon by learners where they have no ownership.

'Learning targets' are more effective in the long term than 'performance targets'

- Performance targets encourage superficial learning, whereas learning targets encourage mastery learning.
- 'Learning targets' are likely to be more motivating for learners.

Provide opportunities for pupils to plan their work

- Superficial planning is likely to lead to superficial work.
- Planning strategies should be explored with children at the start of a topic.
- Teacher's modelling of planning provides evidence of the teacher's willingness to have a go. This demonstrates risk taking.

An objectives-led curriculum can burden teachers and learners

- It tends to restrict the impact of the learner's own experience and prior learning, where this does not fit in with prior teaching objectives.

6 Whole school approaches to learning strategies

> In however friendly and informal a manner, [pupils] are frequently asked to do things, learn things, understand things, for no apparent reason other than that it is what the teacher wants them to do.
>
> (Edwards and Mercer 1987: 158)

This chapter will help you to:

- develop an awareness of learning strategies at a whole school level;
- understand learning strategies in the context of the National Curriculum and the secondary National Strategy framework;
- understand and critique the concepts of 'individualized' and 'personalized' learning.

There has long been rhetoric in favour of independent learning in the English educational establishment. While approaches to learning espoused by curriculum authorities and associated departments may not always be seen as supportive by professionals, there is a long tradition of rhetoric promoting independent learning. Her Majesty's Inspectorate highlighted the importance of independent learning over 20 years ago:

> There is a need for pupils to develop lively enquiring minds, the ability to question and argue rationally . . . to encourage a measure of autonomy [and despite differences of approach], subject matter, levels of abstraction and complexity [in what is taught, this] should not result in a sequence of disparate and unrelated experiences.
>
> (DES 1984, paras 5–8)

Whole school issues in learning

The classroom reality is sometimes far from this ideal. Vygotsky's (1978) zone of proximal development, Bruner's (1986) associated concept of scaffolding, Dweck's (1999) notion of self-theories, Wood's (1998) contingent theory, and Pollard's (1985) model of coping strategies have all been cited as relevant to the analysis of learning strategies in schools. Whatever the labels given to the positions, it is important that factors of both a social and psychological nature are considered.

The following comments illustrate the tensions that reign in many classes:

> Having to 'get through the work'.
> Getting on with each other.
> All of this in a class of 25–30 children.

> There's an awful lot. What I've tried to do, everything to help you out. I've tried to go through all the skills you'll be using next year. Each of those skills you will be using. Audience form and layout. You're trying to persuade people. Your audience. It will be very important next year for your work. This is the last piece of work before next year. Hopefully it will give you an idea about the kind of work that you'll be doing in Y10.
>
> (Year 9 teacher)

The teacher is explaining to her class how the skills which they are currently learning and applying in Year 9 will be useful for them in Key Stage 4 (years 10 and 11). Exams and schools transitions are used as a means of motivation for the children:

> I do want it to be a classroom that's more industrious than it is. I don't think they're working as hard as they could do, especially not on this – on *Macbeth*, it's easier to stand there and almost crack the whip and say, 'You will answer this question', 'We've got to do it. Come on, come on', 'Why do you think that? Why? Why?' and it's easier to crack the whip, almost, and push and push them and get as much work as possible out of them. But other than that I've created work like this . . . used to it and I find it very hard to put them under a lot of pressure. So, really, the atmosphere is changeable.

Clearly, pressure to succeed is keenly felt by this teacher. Pupils, on the other hand, can often see the development of a secure and effective social setting as more important. In the following quote, a pupil sees 'getting on with each other' as an important facet of the classroom, while a relaxed classroom can reduce the perceived pressure of the need to succeed: 'Well, it takes pressure off people because everyone gets on well with each other and you're under less pressure to succeed.' Ultimately pupils make a choice to learn in certain ways based on the learning context engendered by the class teacher and the ethos of the school. In the following extract, a pupil explains to his peer group, be it in a fairly jocular fashion, that he will be leading them in the way that they will tackle a task to dramatize a news report:

Pupil 1: My show, lads, so we play by my rules.
Pupil 2: Yeah, you're the dictator.

The following section describes how independent learning strategies have developed in four secondary schools. It illustrates the range of self-support learning strategies analysed in the four schools included in my research into the use of learning strategies in school.

Learning in four schools

Though schools may have similarities, no two schools are ever the same, nor are individual schools the same in two different years. Though schools operate within a national curriculum in England, they do so in individual ways which respond to the particular needs of their pupils, communities and teachers. Hewitt (2004) focused on learning and the use of learning strategies in four secondary schools. Tasks required of pupils were diverse:

- *School A*: pupils were required to plan a soap opera (with various characters and settings) over two story settings, and then to answer a number of comprehension questions based on an unconnected activity relating to *Romeo and Juliet*.
- *School B*: pupils created a written response to their reading of the novel *Stone Cold* (Swindells 1995). All categories of self-support learning strategies were present in the analysis of observations of this work. Pupils remarked that their teacher had organized their activity in a very detailed way, so that there was little need to confront unexpected problems in completing the written newspaper report on a character from the novel *Stone Cold* (Swindells 1995). What stands out from school B is the emphasis on the class atmosphere, and the contribution this makes to learning. All participants agreed on the 'relaxed' atmosphere in the class, which was considered to be a result of the teacher's style. Pupils felt that this was an important factor in encouraging them to be creative, and for them to use a range of strategies to support their own learning.

- *School C*: this was very different from the other three schools, given that pupils in English were required to work in single-sex classes. Pupils used a range of self-support learning strategies in the creative writing sessions observed. They did, however, say that though their behaviour was atypically quiet, the type of learning and the ways in which they went about it were not significantly different to that of other lessons. The teacher placed a great deal of emphasis on the importance of developing 'confidence'.

- *School D*: this school offered the greatest number of opportunities in lessons for children to use a range of learning strategies. The teacher said that she was quite strict, but had very high expectations of the class. However, she felt that it was very important that she produced motivating activities for them to engage with. She had developed the unit of work based on the Derek Bentley case, in a previous academic year. The unit gave pupils the chance to research aspects of a very controversial case in respect of capital punishment. It had clearly caught the class's attention, and when it came to responding to the issues, they were able to do this in a role-play, which they considered to be very motivating. For this reason, the range of self-support learning strategies used by the pupils is quite diverse. The unit of work was characterized by one lesson focused on evaluation by the pupils, which very successfully enabled them to reflect on the success of their learning. One of the focus pupils was quite different to others from schools A, B and C, in that he saw himself as a class leader. This was very enlightening as to the ways of effective learning, but not necessarily representative of all learners.

There appeared to be no significant differences in the type of self-support strategies used by the pupils. Teachers in all schools spoke about their pupils having a lack of confidence in their abilities in English. Clusters of affective strategies were analysed in all schools. The teachers in all schools highlighted 'classroom atmosphere' as being particularly important. While teachers recognized that they had a large influence on this, they also acknowledged that pupils had the power to change the atmosphere by the roles and actions they adopted. Several teachers considered that their class had previously thrived on a bad reputation, i.e. that the classes had been recognized as having a bad reputation and had appeared to enjoy and propagate this reputation. Teachers said that they had worked very hard with the classes to encourage a more positive ethos. Confidence and self-belief were significant factors in success. In school C, a system of effort evaluation grades had been adopted, English classes were taught in single-sex groups, and overall the teacher felt that the school had gone a long way towards encouraging the pupils:

> Many of the pupils lack the confidence to achieve their potential, this relates in complex ways to the home community and school. The Head Teacher has done a lot for the self-esteem of the pupils in the school. There are a lot of awards at the end of the year but a lot of these are for sports, not so many for academic things.
>
> (Teacher, School C)

Teachers in other schools did not particularly emphasize end-of-year rewards, but they did emphasize the role of the home and community. They saw these as supportive of the school's approach to learning. School D, at parents' evening, would sell dictionaries and thesauruses to encourage pupils to 'work more independently' in English. Though there were pupils who were not motivated in school D, the teacher felt that this was less of a problem compared to other schools she had worked in. In short, she felt that she had to work less hard to motivate the pupils, because they had high aspirations, and valued education as a means to achieve their ambitions.

In all of the discussion above, there has been a strand of concern about the nature of the current curriculum and current underpinning theory. There is great emphasis on the role of instruction in learning (Vygotsky 1978; QCA 1999; DfEE 2001), but less on the role of the learner and the actual process of learning as opposed to teaching. The balance must be regained so that the active nature of the learner is fully recognized and accounted for in the classroom. There is evidence from some participants that without sensitive planning and pedagogical approaches, there is a danger of teaching becoming the end, whereas it is only the means of achieving high quality learning. Of course, any government will want to drive the nature of the curriculum to ensure progress in their own interpretation of 'standards'. But a reconsideration of the role of the learner and self-support learning strategies in the English curriculum will in the long term have a great impact on what counts: the long-term development and success of all pupils' learning.

Developing self-support strategies in the National Curriculum

The following provides an analysis of some recent government curriculum initiatives in England and how they might support the development of active learners employing a range of self-support learning strategies. Examples are taken from recent primary and secondary initiatives. There is much to be positive about in these developments. However, a great deal rests on the professional judgement and skill of the teacher to take the initiative and implement strategies in a way which will be most conducive to the learner.

The Personal, Health, Social and Emotional (PHSE) curriculum and the 'statement of values', in the National Curriculum (QCA 1999), provide the opportunity to focus on the learner: including active approaches to learning and pupils' 'learning values'. In order to implement this aspect of the National Curriculum, schools need to consider their current schemes of work to identify the opportunities for building in explicit units of work in respect of self-support learning strategies. The following suggests some opportunities for the development of learning strategies in the National Curriculum (QCA 1999). The original wording from the National Curriculum is shown in italics. Suggestions for developing learning strategies are shown below:

National Curriculum: Personal Health and Social Education (QCA 1999) Developing confidence and responsibility and making the most of their abilities

'To reflect on and assess their strengths in relation to personality, work and leisure'

- Evaluation by pupils of their use of self-support strategies at home, in the peer group and in the classroom.
- While the focus continues on what pupils learn, increasingly schools should expect them to reflect on how they learn.

'To respect the differences between people as they develop their own sense of identity'

- Role-play and evaluation by pupils of the effective and ineffective use of self-support strategies.

'To recognise how others see them, and be able to give and receive constructive feedback and praise'

- Analysis of effective strategies for working with others (interpersonal and affective self-support learning strategies).
- Use of video material of learners in educational and non-educational settings will help pupils reflect on their own use of learning strategies and to situate their use in a wider context of life-long learning.

National Curriculum: Statement of Values (QCA 1999) The self

'Develop an understanding of our own characters, strengths and weaknesses'

- At the beginning of the year pupils, teachers and the pupils' families themselves should identify the levels of support available for children, including the array of learning strategies encouraged by the various parties.

'Strive, throughout life, for knowledge, wisdom and understanding'

- A personal learning audit should consider the follow features of learning:
  - affective
  - cognitive
  - social
  - learning values.

'Develop self-respect and self-discipline'

- In line with the recommendations of 'assessment for learning', pupils should be expected to contribute to evaluation through self-assessment and peer assessment.

'Clarify the meaning and purpose in our lives and decide, on the basis of this, how we believe that our lives should be lived'

- Teachers and pupils need to identify the value of particular learning strategies for particular units of work.
- Learning mentors could support children in developing targets for how they learn, in addition to what they learn.

'Take responsibility, within our capabilities, for our own lives'

- This will only have an impact on learning if learners are supported in the use of learning strategies which have been negotiated between pupils and their teachers.

'Make responsible use of our talents, rights and opportunities'

- Pupils should be given opportunities to contribute to the planning of new work, so that their perspectives are accounted for in a meaningful curriculum.
- The emphasis should be on encouraging a variety of learning strategies which are responsive to the various demands of school and the wider learning community.

Subject leaders and those responsible for managing the curriculum should re-evaluate their approaches to monitoring teaching and learning to take account of these opportunities. Schools will never succeed in developing pupils' use of independent learning strategies if these are promoted in an isolated way in school. The development and application of independent learning strategies must take place in all subjects and classes.

The Primary National Strategy (DfES 2005) has produced a series of useful materials for developing Social and Emotional Aspects of Learning (SEAL). This develops aspects of the PHSE curriculum through circle time and in cross-curricular learning opportunities. The materials are provided in the form of sets with additional supporting materials centred on particular themes. For example, in Years 3 and 4:

- 'Say no to bullying'
- 'Good to be me'
- 'Changes'
- 'Getting on and falling out'
- 'Relationships'

The materials provide links to assemblies to develop whole-school dimensions to PHSE. There are follow-up activities for pupils to explore the issues in the classroom. 'Say no to bullying', for instance, makes links to lessons in literacy to examine characters and how problem-solving strategies can be used to include other children who are being bullied. Likewise, there are speaking and listening opportunities for reflecting on relationships and issues relating to bullying in their own lives. Interesting links are also made to history by using a picture by Lowry as a stimulus for discussion of bullying. These materials are incredibly useful. They provide opportunities for teachers to develop important aspects of children's learning. Social and affective dimensions are a focus as are more subject-related features. However, the materials do not focus on the affective and social of learning itself. I do believe that these elements are touched on by the materials.

There is no argument at all with the use of these materials. However, I would argue that the social and emotional aspects of learning are intrinsic features of learning and should be the focus of all subject and cross-curricular learning. That the SEAL materials were only developed in 2005, seven years after the introduction of the National Literacy Strategy Framework, provides some evidence of the curricular priorities. Social, emotional and affective aspects of learning must be built into the core and foundation curriculum directly.

All learning is social, affective and emotional and the curriculum needs to incorporate these elements. Additional materials risk being a well-intentioned but passing 'bolt-on' provision to the central curriculum.

Likewise, in primary schools, the development of independent learning strategies through stand-alone 'thinking skills' lessons is unlikely to have a dramatic impact on children's independent learning. Pupils must be encouraged to apply them in other subject areas. In analysing performance data in schools, and setting curricular targets and school improvement plans, there should be a consideration of the use of self-support learning strategies:

- What is the evidence of children's independent learning?
- How have strategies been used by pupils?
- How do school improvement plans support the development of active and self-regulating learners?
- How do targets or individual education programmes support pupils in the development of autonomy?
- If independent learning is not the focus of a school's curriculum, why not?

How a school approaches the notion of independent learning has important implications for the role of the teacher, the learner and learning in the classroom. Could the problem lie with the curriculum and how it is interpreted by the teacher?

Developing self-support strategies in the Key Stage 3 Strategy

By the end of Year 9, the English KS3 Strategy (DfEE 2001) suggests that pupils should be:

- shrewd and fluent independent readers;
- confident writers;
- effective speakers and listeners.

The Key Stage 3 strategy has considered in some depth the question of how teaching and learning can be improved. While there is a substantial range of support materials available for schools, this has been supplemented by considerable professional development opportunities. Features of teaching and learning deemed to be effective have been made explicit through the Key Stage 3 strategy. A reanalysis of the implementation of the Key Stage 3 strategy should consider the place of self-support learning strategies.

The Key Stage 3 Strategy (DfEE 2001) has made great steps towards a consideration of the strategies to encourage effective teaching and learning in secondary English. Hewitt (2004) gives some justification to the framework for an approach to teaching which promotes explicit teaching of learning strategies. This research predates the Key Stage 3 English Strategy by several years. However, the following provides an impetus and theoretical rationale for developing principles of pedagogy and learning in the secondary classroom. Key Stage 3 Strategy advice on teaching is shown in italics with suggestions for relating to the use of learning strategies below:

Teaching according to the KS3 Strategy should be:
'Informed by clear, challenging and progressive objectives'

- The meaning and relevance of objectives should be discussed with pupils.
- They will need to be modified according to the needs of the pupils.
- Relating learning objectives to 'life-long learning' will be important from an early age, if motivation is to be maintained.

'Direct and explicit'

- Teaching should develop pupils' knowledge and understanding of tasks and targets in English (for instance, according to time, quality, quantity and approaches to learning).
- Teachers should investigate the range of learning strategies used by their pupils.
- What do pupils see as the effective use of learning strategies?

'Highly interactive'

- Providing opportunities to explore new areas of learning without pre-conceived ideas of solutions will provide with pupils the chance to learn in exciting and relevant ways.

'Inspiring and motivating'

- Leadership is important from both teachers and pupils in this respect.
- Technology can provide opportunities for making more direct links to the community.
- The business community and projects such as 'Forest school' provide opportunities for exciting learning which inspire children in 'lifelong learning'.
- Developing pupils' use of 'affective' self-support strategies will aid resilience in learning.

'Varied in style and distinguished by a fast pace and strong focus'

- Encourage pupils to use the self-support learning strategies which are appropriate for their learning in English;

- The emphasis should be on fast-paced learning not fast-paced teaching.

'Well-pitched to pupils' needs, inclusive and ambitious'

- Teaching should develop explicit teaching of a range of self-support learning strategies for specific subjects and in cross-curricular learning.
- Teachers should be wary of an overly supportive context and the development of 'learned helplessness'.

Many tools are already available to the teacher to explore their pupils' learning in English, and across the curriculum. *Conferences* between teachers and learners have been used in English for several decades to monitor and record progress in areas such as reading and writing. It would not be a giant leap for teachers to refocus these conferences towards learning, and the use of self-support learning strategies in all aspects of the curriculum. This development has already taken place, in many effective English classrooms, as a result of the Key Stage 3 English Strategy, in the form of *guided group* sessions. In these, the teacher guides pupils through the independent reading or writing of a text, while also reflecting on the learning strategies used by the pupils.

Fisher's (2002) guidance on 'unlocking' literacy considers the strategies pupils might use in understanding a text, including developing the use of *visualization techniques* to develop understanding of characters and settings. Incidentally, this strategy was encouraged quite effectively by the teacher in school C, when developing understanding of characters in narrative writing. Pupils said that they tried to visualize and hear the appearance of characters and their voices.

Developing classroom practice

Educational professionals will need to consider the role of self-support learning strategies throughout the curriculum if they are to re-engage learners in purposeful, reflective and effective learning. Tizard and Hughes (1991) stated that schools fail to engage with the real world because teachers pursue their educational aims without regard to children's perspectives and priorities.

A move to foster self-support learning strategies in pupils would be a significant step in redressing this imbalance.

As a practical step, self-support strategies should be considered in the teacher's introduction to lessons. There is a growing trend among teachers to do the following:

1   write up their learning objectives on the board;
2   discuss these with pupils;
3   identify the success criteria if the pupils are to meet the learning objectives by the end of a lesson or the end of a unit of work;
4   return to these periodically throughout the lesson to refocus pupils' attention on the purposes of the lesson;
5   return to these at the end of the lesson (or more often a longer unit of work over several lessons), in order to carry out an evaluation of the success of the children in meeting these objectives.

The same principle should be encouraged for pupils' use of self-support learning strategies. Teachers should make time to help children recognize the possible strategies (including the affective, cognitive and social dimensions) to support successful learning. Appropriate self-support learning strategies should be identified and made explicit at the start of the lesson. They should be reviewed throughout the lesson, and an evaluation of what worked should take place at the end of the lesson. This will build on much effective practice, which many teachers already implement. It will not, however, be an easy option, as it will require some transfer of responsibility of learning from the teacher to the learner. Some people might argue that a focus on learning outcomes being skewed towards the teacher is a less easy option!

Teachers will also need to reconsider the balance of *learning dilemmas* operating in every class and how they and the pupils will cope within that new situation (Pollard 1985). There is never likely to be a polarized and clear-cut harmony between everyone in class. However, pupils and teachers have the potential to reflect on learning and consider how it may be improved by the use of self-support learning strategies by pupils.

One example alone will illustrate how a more explicit consideration of self-support learning strategies can have a positive impact on the classroom. In earlier chapters I introduced the concept of self-efficacy (Zimmerman 2000): how learners perceive their own learning potential. Pupils should be encouraged to reflect on their perceptions of academic ability. For instance, in Hewitt (2004), many pupils expressed difficulty in writing, even when they were clearly very able compared to others. Developing reflection on the 'affective' dimensions of learning, such as perceived self-efficacy, will help pupils to recognize the potential they possess. Otherwise much energy will be wasted on trying to encourage pupils to engage with writing activities, when pupils are being held back by a lack of motivation for a task or skills which they are clearly capable of achieving. As the saying goes: 'You can lead a horse to water but you can't make it drink.' Though clearly there are complex reasons for a lack of engagement with writing, what a pity it would be if a major barrier was the learner's own negative attitude and self-concept as a barrier to success.

Schools already invest much energy in promoting positive attitudes to writing in the English curriculum. More work is necessary, perhaps along the lines of the writing workshop carried out in school C, where the teacher herself was much more involved in demonstrating her own involvement in the writing process, and the purposes for writing were much more positive from the point of view of the pupils.

There was always some doubt in social constructivist theories about the nature of the individual, choice and free will. Instruction appeared to be something done to an idealized learner, with little consideration of the prior skills, knowledge and learning experiences they bring to the classroom. The theory of self-support strategies explains the pool of resources (skills, knowledge and understandings), which learners might use to facilitate their passage through the zone of proximal development. *The notion of an entirely independent and lone learner operating self-regulatory strategies must be challenged as being a model of effective learning.*

Not all learning is supported by self-support strategies. To that extent, it could be said that ineffective learning may be poorly self-regulated. The less effective learner has little prospect of resolving this position due to the absence of the ability to use self-support learning strategies. None of this is to refute the possibility of a model of self-regulated learning; it does, however, require a reanalysis of the function of learning strategies, and their place in a model of learning.

Personalization of the public services in England has been an influential policy under the influence of New Labour. Lord Adonis and Charles Leadbeatter in the Department for Education and Skills have been particular influential proponents of this policy. Many of the conclusions of this book point towards a greater engagement with the learner, in the same vein as 'personalized learning' (DFES 2006). The Primary National Strategy (2006) offers an example of a curriculum for English and mathematics constructed along such 'personalized' lines. The following section explores the concept of personalized learning, potential difficulties and opportunities.

From individualized teaching to the learning of individuals

Carlgren et al. (2006) include the above phrase in their overview of teaching and learning in Scandinavian schools since the 1960s. This is an interesting starting point to review approaches to the curriculum suggested by recent initiatives in England at the start of the twenty-first century. The concept of 'personalization' has been a driving force. It is worth considering its implications at the level of the school and the local community.

In *Learning about Personalisation: How Can We Put the Learner at the Heart of the Education System?* (DFES 2004b), Charles Leadbeater confronts the issue of how to manage the delivery of a public service (education) to many people in a way which is responsive to them as individuals. He explains:

> All public services are delivered according to a script, which directs the parts played by the actors involved. Many of the scripts followed by public services – such as schooling – have not changed for decades: choose what to study from a pre-defined and delineated set of options; sit with 20–30 other learners; learn from your teacher, who has to deliver set amounts of content often in a particular style; sit some exams; have your learning assessed by an examiner; get your results; move on to the next stage; do it all again. The users are expected to fit into the roles given to them by the script handed down from on high.
>
> (DfES 2004b: 4)

There is an implied promise of a more radical, purposeful and relevant curriculum responsive to individuals, with learners and their communities instrumental in choosing what is relevant to them. However, the following suggests that the 'heavy' hand of centralist government is to be ever present in the design and implementation of the school curriculum:

> At its most basic level, personalisation is about re-writing the education script to make it simpler, more efficient and responsive. Most people want reliable, timely services. They want better basics – it's not rocket science. The charity Barnardo's found this out when they consulted young people on the Green Paper *Every Child Matters* in 2003. When asked to imagine the ideal school, children wanted little more than the absence of various features of schools that blighted their everyday experiences of them. Roofs should not leak, rules should be clear and children ought to be listened to and treated with respect. This isn't about doing anything radically different; it's about doing what you're supposed to be doing better. Ultimately, personalisation could mean providing people with a more customer friendly interface with existing services.
>
> (DFES 2004b: 4)

The concept of 'personalization' seems to oscillate from 'back to better basics' to the politics of 'choice'. The implications for school and curriculum organisation are significant. For instance, Leadbeater (DfES 2004b) suggests that choice in education should focus, among other things, on:

- how to learn;
- what to learn;
- how to be assessed.

Further strategies for developing classroom learning

What are the implications for schools and learners of choice in education? Consider the following models of learning and the questions that they provoke.

Potential arrangements: what to learn

Status quo

- National Curriculum set by central government agency, supported by a list of teaching and learning objectives outlined in more detailed documents (Primary National Strategy and KS3 Strategy documents).

Alternative

- Locally agreed curricular, building on the 'needs' of the community.
- Focus on developing learning strategies.

Implications

- A National Curriculum can be interpreted in a flexible way according to local needs or it can be used tacitly to promote the political ends of a government to the detriment of educational progress of individual children.
- In reality, a locally agreed curriculum could amplify inequalities in communities, such that the 'rich get richer, and the poor get poorer' in educational terms. It could, however, result in much more meaningful learning, with units of work linked to local community and business projects.

Further questions

- In the above scenarios, what are the implications for the development of children's social skills?
- Should social skills form part of the curriculum?
- Who should choose which social skills should be included in the curriculum?
- What message does it give to children, their families and communities where the social skills espoused by the curriculum are at variance with those of the learner?

Potential arrangements: how to learn

Status quo

- Attend a local community school.
- 9.00–3.30 weekday classes.
- Classes of 25–30 children.
- Grouped by 'ability'.

Alternative

- Educational plan (financed centrally) in which learner and their parents draw a learning map.
- E-learning and distance learning options.
- Non-traditional providers of education.
- Learning with others outside of age range, regional or even national boundaries.

Implications

- Strengths of status quo are in the ability of central government to control the quality of the teaching and learning.
- Choice with low expectations could result in a serious decline in 'standards'.
- The gap between school experience of learning and home experience of information and learning is widening in many households.
- A radical shift away from 'traditional school' learning is likely to be inevitable in the long term, as schools find it more and more difficult to maintain behaviour and standards.
- Will a two-tier system of education develop with middle-class parents and more prestigious universities holding onto a traditional view of learning? Meanwhile other groups effectively might opt out of traditional education altogether.

Further questions

- What are the skills of choice and choosing?
- How do learners, families and communities make their 'voices' heard?
- How would learners and their families develop the skills to negotiate the design of a learning experience which they might choose?
- Would different skills develop in response to the different social settings which learners would experience?
- What are the social skills required by future employers?
- How would the social skills required by future employers develop?

Potential arrangements: how to be assessed

Status quo

- Centrally driven 'high stakes' testing such as KS2 and KS3 tests.
- Focus on basic literacy and numeracy skills at primary level.
- Summative assessment results used as a monitoring tool by central government for the purposes of accountability.

Alternative

- Multiplicity of methods, tasks, subject assessments: from which learner chooses.
- Online assessment linked to online learning.
- Emphasis on diagnostic and formative assessment rather than summative assessment.

Implications

- High stakes testing linked to school accountability understandably results in coaching for tests, and ultimately in a diminution of 'real standards' of learning, rather than an increase in centrally set markers of educational standards.
- Local decisions for assessment could result in a plethora of assessment providers with loss of faith in the value of qualifications. Ultimately leading to a reduction in perceived educational standards.

Further questions

- How can schools and other providers of education be made accountable for the performance of learners?
- What should be the balance of summative and formative assessment?
- How much does assessment assess the ability to complete an assessment or the current and potential future levels of learning?
- Is it possible to assess children's ability to learn (learning how to learn)?
- Is it possible or desirable to assess learners' social skills?

Leadbeater provides some insight into what the future school context might be. He emphasizes the notion of a common curriculum which is then applied in different ways by different schools. But, isn't that what happens in English schools at the moment?

Personalised learning would provide children with a greater repertoire of possible scripts for how their education could unfold. At the core there would still be a common script – the basic curriculum – but that script could branch out in many different ways, to have many different styles and endings.

(DfES 2004b: 10)

But a curriculum organized, delivered, experienced and assessed in such different ways risks not being a *national* curriculum at all. In the Introduction to this book, I suggested that schools and policy-makers will always need to make decisions about the balance between accommodation and assimilation in learning; personalization and socialization; and independent and interdependent learning. In the following chapter, I will outline where we are now in these questions and some considerations for the future of school learning.

Summary of implications for the teacher

The use of assessment data as an instrument of accountability can damage learning

- It is likely to develop a performance orientation to learning in both teachers and learners.

Learning objectives should be negotiated between pupils and teachers

- Relating learning objectives to 'lifelong learning' will be important from an early age, if motivation is to be maintained.

Every learning event represents an opportunity to learn about learning

- Develop pupils' knowledge and understanding of tasks and targets in English (for instance, according to time, quality, quantity and approaches to learning).
- Discuss strategies used in successful as well as unsuccessful learning episodes.
- Developing pupils' use of 'affective' self-support strategies will aid resilience in learning.

Emphasize fast-paced learning not fast-paced teaching

- But remember that learners need time and space to reflect in their learning. Otherwise there may be a tendency for shallow and unreflective learning dictated by performance motivation.

Learners should be encouraged to take ownership of their learning

- Planning, choice of learning methods and evaluation all provide opportunities for learners to take responsibility while exercising choice.

Avoid 'learned helplessness'

- Schools should examine trends in the use of learning strategies among their pupils to minimize examples of 'learned helplessness'.
- Training for staff, including Teaching Assistants is very important in avoiding 'learned helplessness'.

Monitoring of effective teaching and learning should shift from an accountability performance model

- For effective lifelong learning, there needs to be a genuine commitment to monitoring learners' use of self-support learning strategies.
- Identification of trends in 'learning values', learning strategies and levels of 'learned helplessness' provides important information about the school as a 'learning community'.
- These elements should feature in a school's self-evaluation and improvement programme.

Make learning links between the school and community

- The business community and projects such as 'Forest school' provide opportunities for exciting learning which inspire children in lifelong learning.
- Many larger companies encourage their employees to take part in classroom projects. Children gain valuable experience from working alongside adults.

7 Conclusion

Standards – developing the (independent and effective learning

> When you go home people don't know and don't care if you're doing home-
> work or if you've got a tutor as long as you don't boast about it. But, like, if
> you're really posh and you act posh in the classroom, showing off, then all the
> other kids hate you.
>
> (Reay 2006: 177)

This chapter will help you to:

- understand the competing priorities of 'socialization' and 'personalization';
- identify ways of planning for learning strategies in the curriculum.

As Reay highlights, children are very aware of how others perceive them as learners. Sometimes the peer group in English primary and secondary schools can view success as a negative. Is this something peculiar to all English schools? Bullock and Muschamp (2006) in their research reveal that there was little negotiation in content or class topics which were dictated by the class teacher. Furthermore, a significant proportion of the children were dissatisfied with this situation.

Reflection

Consider the attitudes towards learning of your class:

- How does the class feel about learning?
- How much control do they exercise over the subject matter and content of the lesson?
- Does choice of topic have an impact on their feelings for learning and confidence abut themselves as learners?
- What other factors influence the learning environment of the class?

Could it be that a lack of control and ownership of learning lead to the develop-ment of negative attitudes in English primary and secondary children?

Strategies for the classroom

Grange Primary School, Long Eaton

This school provides an excellent model for developing pupil voice and governance. No one would claim that this is a perfect school, but it has embraced a very creative and positive approach to the curriculum:

- Pupils elect a child as school mayor.
- The school mayor sits on the governing body of the school.
- Pupils run a radio and TV station, a shop, a museum and an allotment. They manage the production of materials and some of these are sold in the school shop.
- Each of these school facilities is a focus for learning for each of the classes on a carousel basis throughout the year.
- Break times and lunch times are significantly different compared to many other schools. Pupils move freely around the classes according to their interests.

My own experience of the school is that pupils learn with a real purpose, have significant ownership of learning and contribute much to the governance of the school.

Planning for the use of learning strategies

As we have seen in earlier chapters, Zimmerman (2000) outlines a model of self-regulated learning. Zimmerman explains that there are three important influences on the nature of the process of self-regulation: social, environmental and self. Less effective learners tend to use more reactive forms of regulation. For example, when planning a piece of writing, lack of forethought in respect of the intended outcome will often result in a text which fails to use the appropriate language and structures for the intended purpose. The learner will most likely fall back on the feedback from the teacher after marking.

Zimmerman goes on to explain that when the three factors (social, environmental and self), which determine self-regulation are deficient, then this can have an adverse effect on self-regulation. For instance, in a personal experience of visiting a secondary pupil's home to speak to his mother, I was shocked when asking where the boy did his homework to learn that the only object resembling a table in the house was a pool table on which he attempted to do his work. Environmental factors were therefore deficient. Some learners live in an unsupportive family and peer group, where education is not valued. In this case learners are unlikely to be able to call on social factors to support their learning. In terms of learners' views of self, apathy and a lack of interest for school work can exist when they do not accept the worth of an activity in school. This may be due to the distance between the world of the child and the world of the school. In other cases, this may be a simple misunderstanding about the purpose of an activity. These problems would be recognized by most practitioners in the field of education, but how does successful self-regulation develop?

Schunk and Zimmerman (1997) identify four levels in the development of self-regulation:

1   *Observation*: The learner observes the successful use of a strategy by a teacher or more able peer. Thus, for instance, when a teacher demonstrates the writing of certain grammatical structures, this serves as a successful model for pupils in class.
2   *Emulation*: The learner imitates the general pattern or style of a modelled skill. The aim of the learner is to achieve similar motoric and social features of the activity. Rarely will learners be able to achieve exactly the same level of activity, but with the assistance of the teacher or peers, they will be able to achieve similar levels. For instance, when discussing the events, characters and style of a book, a learner may adopt a line of questioning following that of the teacher or peers. This is similar to the development of a community of inquiry suggested by Fisher (1990).
3   *Self-control*: The learner will start to use the skills independently under familiar structured conditions, which have been encountered earlier in the development of the skill. In a drama activity, pupils may develop understanding of a character by the use of hot-seating: a structured activity in which one pupil responds in role from the perspective of a literary character to the questions of others in a group.
4   *Self-regulation*: Only at the point when learners can use a skill or undertake an activity independently across changing personal and environmental conditions, can they be considered to be fully self-regulating. For instance, a learner may have been introduced to the sort of questions which one might ask and try to answer in order to comprehend the themes of a literary text. The ability to carry out such high-level forms of reading comprehension could therefore only said to be properly self-regulating if the learner is able to understand new texts using similar methods. Self-regulation means that the learner chooses what to do, when and how.

Strategies for the classroom

Planning sequences of learning

Use the following template to plan an activity or a sequence of learning in which you plot the development of a learning strategy.

1 Choice of topic and purpose for engaging learning

Examples

- Preparatory session for a unit of work based on group discussion.
- Learners identify areas of need with the support of teacher based on their analysis of previous units of learning.
- Agree an outcome preferably linked to some kind of out-of-school experience such as a school visit or an e-mail link to another school.
- Outcomes should focus on creation in which the learners will have some personal investment: an object, performance, written, screen-based or spoken.

Prompts

- Identify curriculum area from centrally given National Curriculum.
- Learners identify with the help of the teacher links to develop purpose.
- Differentiation by interest from a central topic can be a manageable way for learners to exercise some choice over the work they do.

2 Choice of learning approach

Examples

- Agree how the topic will be explored.
- A presentation by an invited speaker.
- Dramatized simulation of an event or situation.
- An experiment.
- An investigation through books/the library or the Internet.

Prompts

- Learners must employ a range of approaches to learning.
- Avoid just using one or the most popular approach as this will restrict learning strategies in the future.
- Learners should start to develop an awareness of the appropriateness of different approaches to learning.

3 Observation

Examples

- Video of another learner.
- Example of completed work.
- Preferably with other learners explaining strategies which helped them to learn and why they found the skills useful.

Prompts

- Find an example which will demonstrate the skill or learning strategy in use.
- The focus is on cognitive, social and emotional aspects of the skill and activity.

4 Identify learning strategy/strategies

Examples

- Teacher helps learners to understand explicitly the range of strategies helpful in completing the task/sequence of learning.
- Forethought (planning and preparation).
- Performance and control.
- Self-reflection.

Prompts

- At the various stages in the sequence of learning, the teacher and learner should reflect on the appropriate use of learning strategies.
- Various phases of learning do not take place in isolation. Learners will need to review and adjust their strategies and approach to learning as the sequence progresses.

5 Reflection

Examples

- Learner survey, questionnaire or conference to reflect and make explicit the use of learning strategies.
- 'Question exchange' using 'Post-it notes', 'response partners' or a 'graffiti wall' to clarify any misunderstandings.
- 'Learning journal' to make explicit reflections on learning.

Prompts

- Throughout the sequence of learning, it is vital that learners consider their use of learning strategies.
- Reflection should form an integral part of learning, but there is a need to reflect more formally at agreed points in a sequence of learning.

6 Emulation

Examples

- Collaborative planning of an activity or performance of a section of a role-play with support from the teacher based on the previous example.
- Trying to tackle the activity as a whole may be appropriate in some circumstances, but more often than not it will be more motivating for learners to tackle aspects of an activity in manageable stages.

Prompts

- At this stage learners will apply learning strategies to achieve the outcomes established at the outset.
- Learners must be encouraged to apply learning strategies in their own way.
- Learners will always need help to apply these skills at a cognitive, social and affective level.
- While all learning is hard, the skill of the teacher comes in predicting personal and class barriers to learning on as timely a basis as possible.

7 Self-control

Examples

- Read a book to identify themes, characters, setting and develop alternatives which will form part of a story to be read to pupils in another class.

Prompts

- Learners, by exercising some choice in the content and approach to learning, will exercise control from the outset, but they must complete the activity on their own.

8 Self-regulation and evaluation

Examples

- Completion of the task must be carried out by the learner.
- Learners themselves will need to present a piece of writing, carry out a performance, make an object.
- What have the teacher and pupils learned about learning from this sequence?

Prompts

- In planning a sequence of learning there must be sufficient time allowed for pupils eventually to complete and take control of the activity.
- How do the learners feel about the successes and areas for development?
- How do the learners evaluate the success of the teaching and unit of learning?

Reflection on learning strategies

Riding and Rayner (1998) define a learning strategy as a set of one or more procedures that an individual acquires to facilitate the performance on a learning task. Strategies will vary depending on the nature of the task. The above planning template makes reference to affective and social strategies for learning. For example, by encouraging learners to reflect on their motivation and understanding of the purpose of a task, teachers can develop motivation (an affective learning strategy). Nisbet and Shucksmith (1986) suggest that learning strategies go beyond a mere string of learning skills or processes. They are almost always purposeful and goal-orientated, but not necessarily conscious or deliberate. However, in the case of social learning strategies, these may be used on a conscious basis open to investigation. For example, this was highlighted by one child in the research study in respect of group work. Where a child was not participating in a group activity, others said that they encouraged him to give some of his own ideas, which the group then adopted.

The purpose of a sequence of learning is critically important if the learner is to be engaged by the task. Discussion of approaches to learning between the teacher and pupils will help reflection on the strengths and successes of learning, including the use of self-support learning strategies. While Black et al. (2006) acknowledge that learning is not always conscious, they do support explicit reflection on learning, as a way of developing metacognition. Kirby (1984) defines a strategy as a method for approaching a task or more generally attaining a goal. Each strategy would call upon a variety of processes in the course of its operation. Like most concepts in the human sciences, there is 'fuzziness' in the conception of self-support learning strategies. It is suggested, based on the findings of this research, that a learning strategy goes beyond a purely mechanical skill. So, for instance, in designating 'reading' as a cluster of learning strategies, the point has been made that such strategies go beyond mere decoding skills (such as phonics) towards higher-level procedures for investigating a text, such as the use of annotation to highlight the features of characterization in a fiction text.

The teacher invariably sets the goals of any lesson; however, pupils often have choices to make along the way in the process of deciding how they will reach those goals. Affective goals, however, are invariably set by the pupils: this could be in terms of popularity with peers, which will result in greater motivation for engaging with a task, or performance in the longer term. Though exam success was seen as an important goal by teachers, pupils had more personal long-term goals: one pupil in school C said that she wanted to do better than her sister in the GCSE exams (the grade itself was of less importance).

Self-support learning strategies are idiosyncratic to the learner, they may be common to other learners, they may be specific to a curriculum area, or they may be generic (Nisbet and Shucksmith 1986). Self-support learning strategies could be seen like a dialect. On the one hand, a dialect involves groups using common vocabulary and grammar, and learners may adopt the use of common self-support learning strategies: like dialect, this may be a function of class, region or social status, but that may well be taking the metaphor too far. Likewise, individuals operate their own idiosyncratic choice of vocabulary and grammar (an idiolect), and so learners will choose the use their own selection of self-support learning strategies: clearly, a significant difference here is that pupils' ability will have an impact on the range of self-support learning strategies available to them. Pintrich and Schunck (1996) have suggested that more able pupils can use a range of self-regulated learning strategies: in fact, less able pupils can be taught how to use learning strategies to improve their ability to self-regulate, and this will result in higher attainment: there is a long tradition to support this premise, ranging from Brown and Ferrara (1985) to Weinstein et al. (2000). This implies an important link between the use of self-support learning strategies and the content and function of the teaching input. This reflects the essentially social nature of the learning process: the context in which self-support learning strategies develop and operate.

Many teachers acknowledge the importance of the social features of learning. In fact, these elements are frequently cited among their professional concerns. MacNess et al. (2003: 255) highlight tensions within the teaching profession over apparently conflicting areas of focus (Table 7.1).

What counts as 'academic' and what counts as 'affective' is of course open to interpretation. For instance, how would we feel if the headings in Table 7.1 were swapped?

MacNess et al. correctly recognize that the depiction of the issues as two poles should not be interpreted as representing an either/or choice. My point is

Table 7.1 Tensions between academic focus and affective focus

Academic focus		Affective focus
Concern for the 'learner'	versus	Concern for the 'emerging adult'
Subject knowledge	versus	Personal development
High academic achievement	versus	Achievement for citizenship
Discrete subjects	versus	Cross-curricular projects
Individual achievement	versus	Group cooperation
Common levels of achievement	versus	Differentiated teaching
Individualistic autonomy	versus	Collaborative working

that that which is seen as affective actually is necessary for academic success and vice versa. In Chapter 6 I argued for a review of the curriculum to include more emphasis on the social aspects of learning as an end in itself. So, for instance, in the above analysis the ability to work collaboratively is an important end in itself. Employers often cite the ability to work in a team as an essential quality for employees. Individualistic autonomy, on the other hand, has an important affective dimension.

One teacher in Hewitt (2004) saw her principal role as inspiring confidence in her Year 9 English class. The teacher perceived her class as being 'relaxed'. The main motivation for this, she explained, was that her pupils had an 'aversion to risk', and that her job was to set up the atmosphere in the classroom, to give learners the confidence to take risks and be creative:

> Early in September and October they were fairly boisterous . . . It took me about three months to get anything good out of them that was creative. It took me quite a long time to instil some confidence in them in their own ability.
>
> (Teacher)

Teachers frequently refer to the role of confidence in learning. They also highlight the importance of being able to work together. While there are affective and emotional aspects to learning, there is also an important social element. This analysis has been an argument running through this book. Cognition is clearly a very important element in learning, but it should not be seen in isolation from affective and social dimensions. Models of learning which combine these elements to provide an integrated view of learning are much more powerful. For this reason, I would like to argue for a balanced view of learning in which both 'personalization' and 'socialization' are combined in the school curriculum.

Socialization and personalization

In Chapter 6, I explained the political background to notions of personalized learning. In the following section I would like to encapsulate an alternative view in which both 'personalization' and 'socialization' are necessary for a successful experience of learning in schools. On the one hand, we cannot escape from the fact that learners are individuals with their own interests and needs. On the other, we cannot escape the fact that learning happens in a classroom context, involving competing and complex social influences from the peer group, the whole-school ethos and ultimately the wider community within the school.

McNess et al. (2003) contrast a view of teaching as performance compared with competence. They suggest that many of the curriculum and pedagogical developments since the mid-1990s in English primary and secondary schools have encouraged a 'performance' focus on learning. In this approach, high stakes tests have had a significant 'back wash' effect on the curriculum, teaching and learning. The curriculum has narrowed and teachers have become 'deskilled' as a result of 'top down' curriculum initiatives, which have reduced the teachers' ability to mediate between the individual needs of the learner and the school curriculum. As a result, a performance-oriented, transmission model of learning has been given preference over a sociocultural model which recognizes and includes the emotional and social aspects necessary for a more learner-centred approach (Vygotsky 1978). Ultimately pupil learning is less effective when a culture of 'performativity' reigns in the education sector.

> There is a clear tension between the rhetoric of the 'learning society' as represented in English government proposals on lifelong learning (DfEE 1998b), and the reality of the 'performance' culture promoted by current policy-making. The call from national governments for resilient and flexible learners, whose intrinsic motivation will provide the foundation of future economic and social development, will go unanswered unless there is some reduction of current constraints on the exercise of teachers' professional expertise and ability to work creatively with pupils.
>
> (McNess et al. 2003: 256)

While governments continue to provide significant increases in funding for the state-maintained education system in England, as in most countries of the world, it is not surprising that they want some measure of the impact of the funding. However, the use of 'high stakes tests' (for example, KS2 and 3 tests in England) has had a negative influence on the quality of learning in both primary and secondary schools. Yes, the test results provide evidence of the increase in test outcomes, but it is not clear that the overall experience and outcomes of learning have progressed to the degree suggested by statistical analysis of results. Research by UNICEF (reported in the *TES* 2006) suggests that children in the UK rank bottom in the world compared to other countries, rated against six categories of 'well-being' (including material and educational well-being). Asked whether they found their peers 'kind and helpful', only 43 per cent of UK children agreed compared with an international average of 66 per cent. In response, Alan Smithers, Professor of Education at the University of Buckingham, said: 'as well as learning to read and add up, children need to relate to one another and to adults' (*TES* 2006: 11). Is that not a rallying call for the promotion of socialization in schools?

I do not want to paint an overly simplistic picture of the contribution of national policy in England towards socialization: as one in which the

English focus on personalization is absolutely exclusive, rejecting the notion of socialization. Indeed, there is a great deal of praise for DfES inititiatives such as the SEAL materials to support social, emotional aspects of education (DfES 2005). Likewise the Personal, Health and Social education and Citizenship curricular materials have contributed to the development of socialization in primary and secondary schools. These initiatives contribute to areas of personal development such as choice, health issues such as the use of drugs and wider school behavioural issues such as bullying. I do not want to negate the importance of this aspect of the curriculum. However, I would argue that the SEAL materials and the PHSE/Citizenship curriculum are not sufficient in their own right for the development of socialization in primary and secondary schools. I want to argue for a stronger view of socialization.

Socialization is central to all learning

As Guy Claxton (1990) said, every episode of learning is also an opportunity to learn about the process of learning itself. All learning takes place in a social context. Vygotsky (1978) went further by saying that everything which exists on the intra-psychological (psychological) plane first existed on the inter-psychological (sociological) plane. Learning and thinking skills have their roots in the social interactions which take place in formal and informal situations in school.

Returning to MacNess et al. (2003), I would like to argue that a very important way to encourage the development of effective schools is by encouraging the social, affective and emotional aspects of children's learning throughout the day. Classes which are devoid of socialization are devoid of learning. If we really want to encourage purposeful learning and intrinsic motivation, then we must privilege socialization of children in schools.

Does this mean that children must be encouraged to recognize their responsibilities as well as entitlements in school? Yes, it does. Pupils in school are part of a larger whole.

Does it mean that children must be subjugated to the system regardless of their needs? No, but socialization means that learners must develop skills and knowledge co-operatively, which they would not be able to gain on their own. Likewise parents and the community beyond the school gates provide an essential arena within which learning takes place.

We saw in the work of Maddock (2006) in Chapter 3 that much informal but very worthwhile learning occurs outside of school. Schools should help parents to understand that they have a great deal to contribute to a successful learning experience of their children. Socialization occurs when the school supports parents in understanding their particular approaches to learning and how they as parents can contribute to this. Socialization of pupils and parents by the school are both important.

Reflection

Consider the dimensions to learning in your class and school as shown in Table 7.2.

- What elements of personalization and socialization do you perceive in the learning experience offered in your class/school?
- What would be the impact of changes to any one of the dimensions in Table 7.2 to the overall success of the learning and well-being of the children?

There is no single right or wrong answer to the above questions. It is important that schools analyse the characteristics of learning of their pupils. Both socialization and personalization are important if learning is to be effective.

Table 7.2 A comparison 'personalization' and 'socialization' in the classroom

Classroom dimensions	Socialization	Personalization
PLANNING	Collaborative planning between teachers, other teachers, parents and learners	Planning for individual needs
LEARNING	Collaborative learning in pairs, groups and as a whole class, situated in a wider school and community context	Differentiated support for learners of different abilities
TEACHING	Whole class teaching and guided groups	One-to-one support and individualized approaches to learning, for instance, using E-learning opportunities
ASSESSMENT	Group assessments and plenary sessions to identify learning of whole class	Analysis of individual needs and target setting
EVALUATION	Whole class feeback for school councils	Pupil perception surveys
DISCIPLINE	Conforming to whole school rules	School/class adaptations to individual children's behaviour
GOVERNANCE	Whole school ethos through pupil participation and contiribution of school council	Individual contributions to the whole school

---

Strategies for the classroom

Reggio Emilia

An interesting view of the role of socialization can be seen in the approach to education taken in post-war Italy in the area known as Reggio Emilia:

- The teacher's role within the Reggio Emilia approach is complex.
- Working as co-teachers, the role of the teacher is first and foremost to be that of a learner alongside the children.
- The teacher is a teacher-researcher, a resource and guide as she/he lends expertise to children. Within such a teacher-researcher role, educators carefully listen, observe and document children's work and the growth of community in their classroom and are to provoke, co-construct and stimulate thinking, and children's collaboration with peers.

Teachers are committed to reflection about their own teaching and learning. While the cultural and political context of the Reggio Emilia region of Italy may be significantly different from other parts of the world, there are opportunities to take elements of the approach to apply to your own professional context.

Let me here return to a starting point of this book: 'It is teachers who, in the end, will change the world of the school by understanding it' (Stenhouse 1981). *Understanding Effective Learning* is not about providing an off-the-peg template for teachers to apply in their own setting. It is not a silver bullet to cure all ills! This book is about developing understanding of learning.

It is about learners and teachers exercising choice, responsibility and setting out on an exhilarating learning journey. I hope that you enjoy the trip as much as I have done!

Summary of implications for the teacher

Self-regulated learning is determined by social, environmental factors and the self

- The peer group, school context and the learners' perceptions of their own ability will impact on their ability and desire to regulate their learning.

There are four stages in the development of self-regulated learning

- *Observation*: the learner observes the successful use of a strategy by a teacher.

- *Emulation*: the learner imitates the general pattern or style of a modelled skill.
- *Self-control*: the learner will start to use the skills independently under familiar structured conditions.
- *Self-regulation*: only at the point that learners can use a skill or undertake an activity independently across changing personal and environmental conditions, can they be considered to be fully self-regulating.
- Incorporating opportunities for reflection and evaluation enables learners and teachers to consider the use of learning strategies.

Research and understand the use of learning strategies in class and the wider school

- Self-support learning strategies are idiosyncratic to the learner, they may be common to other learners, they may be specific to a curriculum area, or they may be generic.
- The role of the teacher is first and foremost to be that of a learner alongside the children

'Personalization' and 'socialization' are necessary for a successful learning in schools

- Socialization is central to all learning, but the individual perspective is essential if pupils are to be self-regulated.
- Learning and thinking skills have their roots in the social interactions which take place in formal and informal situations in school.

'High stakes' tests have had a significant 'back wash' effect on the curriculum, teaching and learning

- This has led to a performance orientation to learning which has a negative impact on pupil motivation and the quality of their learning.

Glossary

Active learning   Learning is not a passive, knowledge-consuming and externally directed process, but an active, constructive and self-directed process, in which the learner builds up internal knowledge representations that form a personal interpretation of his or her learning experiences (Vermunt 1998).

Contingency (principle of)   The concept of contingent teaching can be extended to cover all strategies used by both teacher and pupils. For instance, effective teaching and learning require the use of strategies only to an appropriate level, to ensure that pupils are making the most effective progress through the zone of proximal development: a balance of challenge and support.

Coping strategies   'a type of patterned and active adaptation to a situation by which an individual copes. It is a creative, but semi-routinised and situational means of protecting the individual's self' (Pollard 1985: 155).

Effective learning   Understanding and conscious reflection on learning strategies are insufficient for effective learning: the learner must know which strategy is right, how to use it and when to use it most appropriately.

Grounded theory   An inductive approach to research, whereby theory develops on an 'a posteriori' basis. Categories and themes are identified in the data, and multiple analyses confirm the status of developing theories (Strauss 1998).

Independent learning   Self-support strategies are important to a reconceptualization of the nature of 'independent learning'. Effective learning, therefore is not self-regulated independent learning, but effective dependent learning, in which the active learner employs an appropriate range of self-support learning strategies, to extract enough support from the physical, cognitive and social environment, for instance, physical resources such as dictionaries; cognitive support such as advice from able peers and the teacher about solving a problem; and social support (such as the development of peer group status by working with other learners).

Learning   There are three kinds of learning: implicit, reactive and deliberative. Implicit learning is where learning is not undertaken in any conscious way, and there is no conscious knowledge of what has been learned. Reactive learning is seen as being near spontaneous in its genesis. The knowledge from this type of learning is only marginally open to conscious interrogation. Deliberative learning takes place in a planned context, and is the most open of informal learning to conscious reflection (Eraut 2000).

Learning about learning 'Every learning experience is not only an invitation to improve our theories about the world; it is also an opportunity to improve our implicit theories about theory-building: to become a better learner' (Claxton 1990: 101).

Learning strategies Learning strategies are therefore procedures of a cognitive, affective, social or moral nature, which the learner adopts to carry out an activity in the classroom, in order to participate and work towards an activity, in order to achieve a short- or longer-term goal set by themselves or the teacher.

Learning styles 'an individual set of differences that include not only a stated personal preference for instruction or an association with a particular form of learning activity, but also individual differences found in intellectual and personal psychology' (Riding and Rayner 1998).

Network of interdependencies Social network of dependencies: effective learners support each other and this builds up social credit within the peer group: social construction of self (Demetriou 2000).

Self 'The essence of the self, as we have said, is cognitive: it lies in the internalised conversation of gestures, which constitute thinking, or in terms of which thought or reflection proceeds. And hence the origin and the foundations of the self, like those of thinking, are social' (Mead 1934).

Self-regulation 'A social cognitive perspective differs markedly from theoretical traditions, which define self-regulation as a singular internal state, trait or stage that is genetically endowed or discovered. Instead it is defined in terms of context-specific processes that are used cyclically to achieve personal goals. These processes entail more than metacognitive knowledge and skill; they also include affective and behavioural processes, and a resilient sense of self-efficacy to control them' (Zimmerman 2000: 14).

Self-support learning strategies Self-support learning strategies are the affective, social and cognitive strategies which pupils use to support their development in new areas of learning. While the teacher lends support for an activity, the effective learner will adopt self-support strategies to facilitate their passage through the zone of proximal development: by lending positive support to the instructional input, or where the teacher input is not appropriate, self-support strategies are used to mediate in order to ensure a more appropriate form of instructional input.

Self-supported learning Self-supported learning enables a learner to complete activities when the learning expected is beyond their level of development: hence beyond their current level of self-regulation.

Validity The concept of validity involves validation of the craftsmanship, a dialogue between the participants of the research (including the researcher), and validation of the application of the research (Kvale 2002).

Bibliography

Adelman, C., Jenkins, D. and Kemmis, S. (1980) Rethinking case study: notes from the Second Cambridge Conference, in H. Simons (ed.) *Towards a Science of the Singular*. University of East Anglia: Centre for Applied Research in Education.

Alexander, R., Rose, J. and Woodhead, C. (1993) The quality of teaching in primary schools, in R. Gomm and P. Woods (eds) *Educational Research in Action*. Milton Keynes: Open University Press.

Andersson, S. and Andersson, I. (2005) Authentic learning in a sociocultural framework: a case study on non-formal learning, *Scandinavian Journal of Educational Research*, 49(4): 419–36.

Ausubel, D.P. (1958) *Theory and Problem of Child Development*. New York: Grune & Stratton.

Ball, S.J. (1991) Power, conflicts, micropolitics and all that! In G. Walford (ed.) *Doing Educational Research*. New York: Routledge.

Baron, J. (1978) Intelligence and general strategies, in G. Underwood (ed.) *Strategies of Information Processing*. London: Academic Press.

Bassey, M. (1981) Pedagogic research: on the relative merits of the search for generalization and study of single events, *Oxford Review of Education*, 7(1): 73–93.

Baumfield, B. (2006) Tools for pedagogical inquiry: the impact of teaching thinking skills on teachers, *Oxford Review of Education*, 32(2): 185–96.

Beck, R.N. (1979) *Handbook in Social Philosophy*. New York: Macmillan.

Bell, J. (1999) *Doing Your Research Project: A Guide for the First-time Researcher in Education and Social Science*. Milton Keynes: Open University Press.

Belmont, J.M. (1989) Cognitive strategies and strategic learning, *American Psychologist*, 44(2): 142–8.

Bennett, N. (1989) Changing perspectives on teaching-learning processes in the post-Plowden era, in P. Murphy and B. Moon (eds) *Developments in Learning and Assessment*. London: Hodder & Stoughton.

Black, P., McCormick, R., James, M. and Pedderd, D. (2006) Learning how to learn and assessment for learning: a theoretical inquiry, *Research Papers in Education*, 21(2): 119–32.

Black, P., Swann, J. and Wiliam, D. (2006) School pupils' beliefs about learning, *Research Papers in Education*, 21(2): 151–70.

Black, P. and Wiliam, D. (1998) Assessment and classroom learning, *Assessment in Education*, 5(1): 7–73.

Boaler, J. (1997) Setting, social class and survival of the quickest, *British Educational Research Journal*, 23(5): 575–95.

Bokaerts, M. (ed.) (2000) *Handbook of Self-regulation*. New York: Academic Press.

Bouffard, T., Vezeau, C. and Bordeleau, L. (1998) A developmental study of the relation between combined learning and performance goals and students' self-regulated learning, *British Journal of Educational Psychology*, 68: 309–19.

Brice-Heath, S. (1983) *Ways with Words*. Cambridge: Cambridge University Press.

Britton, J. (1970) *Language and Learning*. London: Penguin.

Brown, A.L. (1974) The role of strategic behaviours in retardate memory, in N.R. Ellis (ed.) *International Review of Research in Mental Retardation*. New York: Academic Press.

Brown, A.L. (1977) Development, schooling and the acquisition of knowledge about knowledge, in R.C. Anderson, R.J. Spiro and W.E. Montague (eds) *Schooling and the Acquisition of Knowledge*. Hillsdale NJ: Erlbaum.

Brown, A.L. and Campione, J.C. (1979) Inducing flexible thinking: the problem of access, in M.P. Friedman, J.P. Das and N. O'Connor (eds) *Intelligence and Learning*. New York: Plenum Press.

Brown, A.L. and Ferrara, R.A. (1985) Diagnosing zones of proximal development, in J.V. Wertsch (ed.) *Culture, Communication and Cognition: Vygotskyan Perspectives*. Cambridge: Cambridge University Press.

Brown, J. and Sime, J.D. (1981) A methodology of accounts, in M. Brenner (ed.) *Social Method and Social Life*. London: Academic Press.

Bruner, J. (1985) Vygotsky: a historical and conceptual perspective, in J.V. Wertsch (ed.) *Culture, Communication and Cognition: Vygotskyan Perspectives*. Cambridge: Cambridge University Press.

Bruner, J. (1986) *Actual Minds, Possible Worlds*. Cambridge, MA: Harvard University Press.

Bullock, K., and Muschamp, Y. (2006) Learning about learning in the primary school, *Cambridge Journal of Education*, 36(1): 49–62.

Burgess, T. (1993) Reading Vygotsky, in H. Daniels (ed.) *Charting the Agenda: Educational Activity after Vygotsky*. London: Routledge.

Burns, C. and Myhill, D. (2004) Interactive or inactive? A consideration of the nature of interaction in whole class teaching, *Cambridge Journal of Education*, 34(1).

Butterfield, E.C. and Belmont, J.M. (1977) Assessing and improving the executive cognitive functions of mentally retarded people, in I. Bailer and M. Steinlicht (eds) *Psychological Issues in Mental Retardation*. Chicago: Aldine Press.

Camp, B. and Bash, M.B. (1980) Developing self-control through training in problem solving: the 'Think aloud' program, in D. Pickett-Rathjen and J.P. Foreyt (eds) *Social Competence: Intervention for Children and Adults*. Oxford: Pergamon.

Candy, P. (1988) On the attainment of subject-matter autonomy, in D. Boud (ed.) *Developing Student Autonomy in Learning*. London: Kogan Page.

Carlgren, I., Klette, K., Myrdal, S., Schnack, K. and Simola, H. (2006) Changes in

Nordic teaching practices: from individualised teaching to the teaching of individuals, *Scandinavian Journal of Educational Research*, 50(3): 301–26.

Caspi, A., McClay, J., Moffitt, T.E., Mill, J., Martin, J., Craig, I.W., Taylor, A. and Poulton, R. (2002) Role of genotype in the cycle of violence in maltreated children, *Science*, 297: 851–4.

Chilver, P. and Gould, G. (1982) *Language and Learning in the Classroom: Discursive Talking and Writing across the Curriculum.* Oxford: Pergamon.

Chomsky, N.A. (1965) *Aspects of the Theory of Syntax.* Cambridge, MA: MIT Press.

Claxton, G. (1990) *Teaching to Learn.* London: Cassell.

Cohen, L. and Manion, L. (1994) *Research Methods in Education*, 4th edn. London: Routledge.

Cole, M. (1985) The zone of proximal development: where culture and cognition create each other, in J.V. Wertsch (ed.) *Culture, Communication and Cognition: Vygotskyan Perspectives.* Cambridge: Cambridge University Press.

Cossentino, J. (2006) Big work: goodness, vocation, and engagement in the Montessori method, *Curriculum Inquiry*, 36(1): 63–92.

Crawford, R. (1999) Teaching and learning IT in secondary schools: towards a new pedagogy? *Education and Information Technologies*, 4: 49–63.

Cremin, H., Thomas, G. and Vincett, K. (2005) Working with teaching assistants: three models evaluated, *Research Papers in Education*, 20(4): 413–32.

Czerniewska, P. (1992) *Learning about Writing: The Early Years.* Oxford: Blackwell.

Daniels. H. (ed.) (1993) *Charting the Agenda: Educational Activity after Vygotsky.* New York: Routledge.

Dann, R. (2002) *Promoting Assessment as Learning: Improving the Learning Process.* London: Routledge Falmer.

Davies, T. (2006) Creative teaching and learning in Europe: promoting a new paradigm, *The Curriculum Journal*, 17(1): 37–57.

Delamont, S. and Hamilton, D. (1986) Revisiting classroom research: a continuing cautionary tale, in M. Hammersley (ed.) *Controversies in Classroom Research.* Milton Keynes: Open University Press.

Demetriou, A. (2000) Organisation and development of self-understanding and self-regulation: towards a general theory, in M. Bokaerts (ed.) *Handbook of Self-regulation.* New York: Academic Press.

Denscombe, M. (1998) *The Good Research Guide.* Buckingham: Open University Press.

Denzin, N.K. (1989) *Interpretive Biography.* London: Sage.

DES (1975) *Language for Life: Report on the Bullock Committee.* London: HMSO.

DES (1984) *Education Observed.* London: HMSO.

DES (1995) *Revised National Curriculum: English.* London: HMSO.

Dewey, J. (1900) Psychology and social practice, *Psychological Review*, 7: 105–24.

DfEE (1998a) *Framework for the National Literacy Strategy.* London: HMSO.

DfEE (1998b) *Report on the Task Force Report on the National Literacy Project.* London: HMSO.

DfEE (2001) *Framework for Teaching English: Year 7, 8 and 9*. London: HMSO.

DfES (2003) *Excellence and Enjoyment: A Strategy for Primary Schools*. London: HMSO.

DfES (2004a) *Every Child Matters: Change for Children*. London: HMSO.

DfES (2004b) *Learning about Personalization: How Can We Put the Learner at the Heart of the Education System?* London: HMSO.

DfES (2005) *Social and Emotional Aspects of Learning . . . Improving Behaviour . . . Improving Learning*. London: HMSO.

DfES (2006) *Primary Framework for Literacy and Mathematics*. London: HMSO.

Donaldson, M. (1978) *Children's Minds*. London: Fontana.

Duff, A. (1997) A note on the reliability and validity of a 30-item version of Entwistle and Tait's Revised Approaches to Studying Inventory, *British Journal of Educational Psychology*, 67: 529–39.

Dweck, C.S. (1999) *Self-theories: Their Role in Motivation, Personality, and Development*. Cardiff: Psychology Press.

Edwards, D. and Mercer, N. (1987) *Common Knowledge: The Development of Understanding in the Classroom*. London: Methuen.

Einstein, A. and Infield, L. (1938) *The Evolution of Physics*. New York: Oxford University Press.

Eisner, E. (1993) Objectivity in educational research, in M. Hammersley, (ed.) *Educational Research: Current Issues*. Milton Keynes: Open University Press.

Entwistle, N.J. (ed.) (1985) *New Directions in Educational Psychology: Learning and Teaching*. Sussex: Falmer Press.

Entwistle, N.J. (1987) *Understanding Classroom Learning*. London: Hodder & Stoughton.

Entwistle, N.J. and Hutchinson, C. (1985) Question difficulty and the concept of attainment, in N.J. Entwistle (ed.) *New Directions in Educational Psychology*. Vol. 1 *Learning and Teaching*. Sussex: Falmer Press.

Entwistle, N.J. and Koseki, B. (1985) Relationships between school motivation, approaches to studying and attainment, *British Journal of Educational Psychology*, 55(2): 124–37.

Eraut, M. (2000) Non-formal learning and tacit knowledge in professional work, *British Journal of Educational Psychology*, 70: 113–36.

Fisher, R. (1990) *Teaching Children to Think*. New Jersey: Simon and Schuster.

Fisher, R. (2002) *Unlocking Literacy: A Guide for Teachers*. London: David Fulton.

Flavell, J.H. (1976) Metacognitive aspects of problem solving, in L.B. Resnick (ed.) *The Nature of Intelligence*. Hillsdale, NJ: Erlbaum.

Flavell, J.H. (1981) Cognitive monitoring, in W.P. Dickson (ed.) *Children's Oral Communication Skills*. New York: Academic Press.

Flavell, J.H. and Wellman, H.M. (1977) Metamemory, in R.V. Kail and J.W. Hagen (eds) *Perspectives on the Development of Memory and Cognition*. Hillsdale, NJ: Erlbaum.

Flutter, J. (2006) 'This place could help you learn': student participation in creating better school environments, *Educational Review*, 58(2): 183–93.

Fontana, A. and Frey, J.H. (1994) Interviewing: the art of science, in N.K. Denzin and Y.S. Lincoln (eds) *Handbook of Qualitative Research*. London: Sage.

Fox, R. (1982) Thinking and the language arts, in P. Chilver and G. Gould (eds) *Language and Learning in the Classroom: Discursive Talking and Writing across the Curriculum*. Oxford: Pergamon.

Fuson, K.C. (1985) The development of self-regulating aspects of speech: a review, in J.V. Wertsch (ed.) *Culture, Communications and Cognition: Vygotskyan Perspectives*. Cambridge: Cambridge University Press.

Gagné, R.M. (1977) *The Conditions of Learning*. New York: Holt, Rinehart & Winston.

Galton, M. (1989) *Teaching in Primary Classrooms*. London: David Fulton Publishers.

Galton, M., Hargreaves, L., Comber, C., Wall, D. and Pell, T. (1999) Changes in patterns of teacher interaction in primary classrooms: 1976–96, *British Educational Research Journal*, 25(1): 23–37.

Gardner, H. (1999) *Intelligence Reframed: Multiple Intelligences for the 21st Century*. New York: Basic Books.

Garner, R. (1988) Verbal report data on cognitive and metacognitive strategies, in C.E. Weinstein, E.T. Goetz and P.A. Alexander (eds) *Learning and Study Strategies: Issues in Assessment, Instruction and Evaluation*. San Diego: Academic Press.

Geisler-Brenstein, E., Schmeck, R.R. and Hetherington, J. (1996) An individual difference perspective on student diversity, *Higher Education*, 31: 73–96.

Gillies, R.M. (2000) The maintenance of cooperative and helping behaviours in cooperative groups, *British Journal of Educational Psychology*, 70: 91–111.

Giordmaina, J. (1999) Communities of conversation in 'Philosophy for Children' programmes, paper presented at British Educational Research Association Annual Conference, University of Sussex, Brighton.

Goswami, U. (2004) Neuroscience, education and special education, *British Journal of Special Education*, 31(4): 175–83.

Hardman, F., Smith, F. and Wall, K. (2005) Teacher–pupil dialogue with pupils with special educational needs in the National Literacy Strategy, *Educational Review*, 57(3): 299–315.

Hargreaves, A. (1984) The significance of classroom strategies, in A. Hargreaves and P. Woods (eds) *Classrooms and Staff-rooms*. Milton Keynes: Open University Press.

Hargreaves, E. (2005) Assessment for learning? Thinking outside the (black) box, *Cambridge Journal of Education*, 35(2): 213–24.

Harlen, W. and Crick, R. (2003) Testing and motivation for learning, *Assessment in Education*, 10(2): 169–207.

Harrison, C. (2005) Teachers developing assessment for learning: mapping teacher change, *Teacher Development*, 9(2): 255–64.

Harter, S. (1990) Causes, correlates, and the functional role of global self-worth: a life-span perspective, in R. Sternberg and J. Kolligan (eds) *Competence Considered*. New Haven, CT: Yale University Press.

Hartley, D. (2006) Excellence and enjoyment: the logic of a 'contradiction', *British Journal of Educational Studies*, 54(1): 3–14.

Hatch, T., Eiler White, M. and Capitelli, S. (2005) Learning from teaching: what's involved in the development of classroom practice? *Cambridge Journal of Education*, 35(3): 323–31.

Hewitt, D. (1999) Self-support strategies in Year 9 English classes, a paper delivered at the British Educational Research Association's Annual Conference (student symposium) in Brighton, Sussex, September.

Hewitt, D. (2004) Self-support strategies in Year 9 English classes, PhD thesis, University of Derby.

Hewitt, D. and Mellar, L. (1999) *A Comparison of Reading in Year 6 and Year 7 Classes*. London: TTA.

Hilton, M. (1998) Raising literacy standards: the true story, *English in Education*, 32(3): 33–43.

Honess, T. and Yardley, K. (1987) *Self and Identity: Perspectives across the Lifespan*. New York: Routledge and Kegan Paul.

Houtz, J.C. (1994) Creative problem solving in the classroom: contributions of four psychological approaches, in M.A. Runco (ed.) *Problem Solving, Problem Finding and Creativity*. New Jersey: Ablex.

James, M. (2000) Measured lives: the rise of assessment as the engine of change in English schools, *The Curriculum Journal*, 11(3): 343–64.

James, M., Black, P., McCormick, R., Pedder, D. and Wiliam, D. (2006) Learning how to learn, in classrooms, schools and networks: aims, design and analysis, *Research Papers in Education*, 21(2): 101–18.

James, M. and Pedder, D. (2006) Beyond method: assessment and learning practices and values, *The Curriculum Journal*, 17(2): 109–38.

James, W. (1892) *Psychology: The Briefer Course*. New York: Henry Holt.

Jausovec, N. (1994) Metacognition in creative problem solving, in M.A. Runco (ed.) *Problem Solving, Problem Finding and Creativity*. New Jersey: Ablex.

Jeffrey, B. (2003) Countering learner 'instrumentalism', *British Educational Research Journal*, 29(4): 489–504.

John-Steiner, V. (1985) The road to competence in an alien land: a Vygotskian perspective on bilingualism, in J.V. Wertsch (ed.) *Culture, Communication and Cognition: Vygotskyan Perspectives*. Cambridge: Cambridge University Press.

Kane, R. and Maw, N. (2005) Making sense of learning at secondary school: involving students to improve teaching practice, *Cambridge Journal of Education*, 35(3): 311–22.

Kaplan, A. (1973) *The Conduct of Inquiry*. Aylesbury: Intertext Books.

Katz, I., Assor, A., Kanat-Maymon, Y. and Bereby-Meyer, Y. (2006) Interest as a motivational resource: feedback and gender matter, but interest makes the difference, *Social Psychology of Education*, 9: 27–42.

Kavale, K. A. and Forness, S. R. (1987) Substance over style: assessing the efficacy of modality testing and teaching, *Exceptional Children*, 54(3): 228–39.

Kirby, J.R. (ed.) (1984) *Cognitive Strategies and Educational Performance*. New York: Academic Press.

Kitwood, T.M. (1977) Values in adolescent life: towards a critical description, unpublished PhD dissertation, University of Bradford, School of Research in Education.

Klein, P. (2003) Rethinking the multiplicity of cognitive resources and curricular representations: alternatives to 'learning styles' and 'multiple intelligences', *Journal of Curriculum Studies*, 35(1): 45–81.

Kozeki, B. (1985) Motives and motivational styles in education, in N.J. Entwistle (ed.) *New Directions in Educational Psychology: Learning and Teaching*. Sussex: Falmer Press.

Kuiper, R. and Pesut, D. (2004) Promoting cognitive and metacognitive reflective reasoning skills in nursing practice: self-regulated learning theory. Issues and innovations in nursing education, *Journal of Advanced Nursing*, 45(4): 381–91.

Kutnick, P., Blatchford, P. and Baines, E. (2005) Grouping of pupils in secondary school classrooms: possible links between pedagogy and learning, *Social Psychology of Education*, 8: 349–74.

Kvale, S. (2002) The social construction of validity, in N.K. Denzin and Y.S. Lincoln (eds) *The Qualitative Inquiry Reader*. London: Sage Publications.

Lacey, C. (1993) Problems of sociological fieldwork: a review of the methodology of *Hightown Grammar*, in M. Hammersley (ed.) *Educational Research: Current Issues*. Milton Keynes: Open University Press.

Lahtinen, V., Lonka, K. and Lindblom-Ylanne, S. (1997) Spontaneous study strategies and the quality of knowledge construction, *British Journal of Educational Psychology*, 67: 13–24.

Lankshear, C. and Knobel, M. (2004) *A Handbook for Teacher Research: From Design to Implementation*. Milton Keynes: Open University Press.

Lawson, M. (1980) Meta-memory: making decisions about strategies, in J.R. Kirby and J.B. Biggs (eds) *Cognition, Development and Instruction*. London: Academic Press.

Licht, B.G. and Dweck, C.S. (1984) Sex differences in achievement orientations: consequences for academic choices and attainments, in M. Marland (ed.) *Sex Differentiation and Schooling*. London: Heinemann.

Lincoln, Y.S. (2002) Emerging criteria for quality in qualitative and interpretive research, in N.K. Denzin and Y.S. Lincoln (eds) *The Qualitative Inquiry Reader*. London: Sage Publications.

Maddock, M. (2006) Children's personal learning agendas at home, *Cambridge Journal of Education*, 36(2): 153–69.

Markus, H. and Wurf, E. (1987) The dynamic self-concept: a social psychological perspective, *Annual Review of Psychology*, 38: 299–337.

Marshall, B. and Drummond M.J. (2006) How teachers engage with Assessment for Learning: lessons from the classroom, *Research Papers in Education*, 21(2): 133–49.

Mayer, R.E. (1983) *Thinking, Problem Solving, Cognition*. New York: Freeman and Co.

McAllister, W. (1995) Are pupils equipped for group work without training or instruction? *British Educational Research Journal*, 21(3): 395–404.

McCombs, B.L. (1988) Motivational skills training: combining metacognitive, cognitive, and affective learning strategies, in C.E. Weinstein, E.T. Goetz and P.A. Alexander (eds) *Learning and Study Strategies: Issues in Assessment, Instruction and Evaluation*. San Diego: Academic Press.

McGuiness, C. and Nisbet, J. (1990) Teaching thinking in Europe, *British Journal of Educational Psychology*, 61: 174–86.

McNamee, M. and Bridges, D. (2002) *The Ethics of Educational Research*. London: Blackwell.

McNess, E., Broadfoot, P. and Osborn, M. (2003) Is the effective compromising the affective? *British Educational Research Journal*, 29(2): 243–58.

Mead, G.H. (1934) *Mind, Self and Society*. Chicago: University of Chicago Press.

Meadows, S. (1993) *The Child as Thinker: The Development and Acquisition of Cognition in Childhood*. London: Routledge.

Mercer, N. (1991) Researching common knowledge: studying the content and context of educational discourse, in G. Walford (ed.) *Doing Educational Research*. New York: Routledge.

Mercer, N., Wegerif, R. and Dawes, L. (1999) Children's talk and the development of reasoning in the classroom, *British Educational Research Journal*, 25(1): 95–111.

Mitsoni, F. (2006) 'I get bored when we don't have the opportunity to say our opinion': learning about teaching from students, *Educational Review*, 58(2): 159–70.

Murphy, N. and Messer, D. (2000) Differential benefits from scaffolding and children working alone, *Educational Psychology*, 20(1): 17–31.

Myhill, D. (2006) Talk, talk, talk: teaching and learning in whole class discourse, *Research Papers in Education*, 21(1): 19–41.

Myhill, D. and Warren, P. (2005) Scaffolds or straitjackets? Critical moments in classroom discourse, *Educational Review*, 57(1).

Nisbet, J. and Shucksmith, J. (1986) *Learning Strategies*. London: Routledge and Kegan Paul.

Noddings, N. (2005) Identifying and responding to needs in education, *Cambridge Journal of Education*, 35(2): 147–59.

Norman, K. (1992) *Thinking Voices: The Work of the National Oracy Project*. London: Hodder & Stoughton.

OFSTED (1996) *Teaching of Reading in 45 London Primary Schools*. London: HMSO.

Ommundsen, Y., Haugen, R. and Lund, T. (2005) Academic self-concept, implicit theories of ability, and self-regulation strategies, *Scandinavian Journal of Educational Research*, 49(5): 461–74.

Palinscar, A.S. and Brown, A.L. (1984) Reciprocal teaching of comprehension-fostering and comprehension-monitoring activities, *Cognition and Instruction*, 1: 117–75.

Pangagopoulou-Stamatelatou, A. and Merrett, F. (1996) Improving children's writing: the construction of a behavioural self-management package, *British Educational Research Journal*, 22(2): 207–22.

Paris, C. and Combs, B. (2006) Lived meanings: what teachers mean when they say they are learner-centered, *Teachers and Teaching: Theory and Practice*, 12(5): 571–92.

Paris, S.G. (1988) Models and metaphors of learning strategies, in C.E. Weinstein, E.T. Goetz and P.A. Alexander *Learning and Study Strategies: Issues in Assessment, Instruction and Evaluation*. San Diego: Academic Press.

Parsons, A., Frydenberg, E. and Poole, C. (1996) Overachievement and coping strategies in adolescent males, *British Journal of Educational Psychology*, 66: 109–14.

Paulsen, E., Bru, E. and Murberg, T. (2006) Passive students in junior high school: the associations with shyness, perceived competence and social support, *Social Psychology of Education*, 9: 67–81.

Perrenoud, P. (1998) From formative evaluation to a controlled regulation of learning processes: towards a wider conceptual field, *Assessment in Education*, 5(1): 85–102.

Piepho, H. (1978) Some psychological bases for learning strategies and exercises in the communicative teaching of English, in C.N. Candlin (ed.) *The Communicative Teaching of English*. London: Longman.

Pintrich, P.R. and Schunk, D.H. (1996) *Motivation in Education: Theory, Research and Applications*. Englewood Cliffs, NJ: Prentice-Hall.

Pollard, A. (1982) A model of classroom coping strategies, *British Journal of Sociology of Education*, 3(1): 19–37.

Pollard, A. (1985) *The Social World of the School*. London: Holt, Rinehart & Winston.

Pollard, A. (1988) *Sociology and Teaching*. London: Croom Helm.

Pollard, A. (1998) *Reflective Practice in the Primary School*, 3rd edn. London: Routledge.

Postlethwaite, K. and Haggarty, L. (1998) Towards effective and transferable learning in secondary school: the development of an approach based on mastery learning, *British Educational Research Journal*, 24(3): 333–54.

Pressley, M., Woloshyn, V. and Associates (1995) *Cognitive Strategy Instruction that Really Improves Children's Academic Performance*, 2nd edn. Cambridge, MA: Brookline Books.

QCA (1999) *National Curriculum*. London: HMSO.

Reay, D. (2006) 'I'm not seen as one of the clever children': consulting primary school pupils about the social conditions of learning, *Educational Review*, 58(2): 171–81.

Reinberg, F., Vollmeyer, R. and Wollett, F. (2000) Motivation and action in self-regulated learning, in M. Bokaerts (ed.) *Handbook of Self-Regulation*. New York: Academic Press.

Resnick, L. and Beck, I.L. (1976) Designing instruction in reading: interaction of theory and practice, in J.T. Guthrie (ed.) *Aspects of Reading Acquisition*. Baltimore, MD: Johns Hopkins University Press.

Riding, R.J. and Buckle, C.F. (1990) *Learning Styles and Training Performance*. Sheffield: Training Agency.

Riding, R.J., Burton, D., Rees, G. and Sharratt, M. (1995) Cognitive Style and personality in 12-year-old children, *British Journal of Educational Psychology*, 65: 113–24.

Riding, R.J. and Dyer, V.A. (1980) The relationship between extraversion and verbal-imagery learning style in 12-year-old children, *Personality and Individual Differences*, 1: 273–79.

Riding, R.J. and Rayner, S.G. (1998) *Cognitive Styles and Learning Strategies*. London: David Fulton Publishers.

Roberts R.N. (1979) Private speech in academic problem-solving: a naturalistic perspective, in G. Zivin, *The Development of Self-regulation through Private Speech*. New York: John Wiley.

Robinson, E.J. and Robinson, W.P. (1982) The advancement of children's verbal referential communication skills: the role of metacognitive guidance, *International Journal of Behavioural Development*, 5: 329–55.

Root, A. (1981) Working with a colleague, in J. Nixon (ed.) *A Teacher's Guide to Action Research*. London: Grant McIntyre.

Rosen, M. and Oxenbury, H. (1993) *We're Going on a Bear Hunt*. London: Walker Books.

Runco, M.A. and Chand, I. (1994) Problem finding, evaluative thinking and creativity, in M.A. Runco (ed.) *Problem Solving, Problem Finding and Creativity*. New Jersey: Ablex.

Rutter, M. (1975) *Helping Troubled Children*. London: Penguin.

Sanger, J. (1995) Five easy pieces: the deconstruction of illuminatory data in research writing, *British Educational Research Journal*, 21(1): 89–97.

Sapsford, R.J. and Evans, J. (1984) Evaluating a research report, in J. Bell, T. Bush and A. Fox et al. (eds) *Conducting a Small-scale Investigation in Educational Management*. London: Harper & Row.

Schallert, D.L. and Kleiman, G.M. (1979) *Some Reasons Why the Teacher is Easier to Understand than the Textbook*. Chicago: University of Illinois.

Schmeck, R.R. (1988) Individual differences and learning strategies, in C.E. Weinstein, E.T. Goetz and P.A. Alexander *Learning and Study Strategies: Issues in Assessment, Instruction and Evaluation*. San Diego: Academic Press.

Schoenfeld, A.H. (1988) When good teaching leads to bad results: the disaster of well-taught maths courses, *Educational Psychologist*, 23: 145–66.

Schön, D.A. (1983) *The Reflective Practitioner*. New York: Basic Books.

Schunk, D.H. and Ertmer, P.A. (2000) Self-regulation and academic learning: self-efficacy enhancing interventions, in M. Bokaerts (ed.) *Handbook of Self-regulation*. New York: Academic Press.

Schunk, D.H. and Zimmerman, B.J. (1997) Social origins of self-regulatory competence, *Educational Psychologist*, 32: 195–208.

Seifert, J., Scheuerpflug, P., Zillessen, K. E., Fallgater, A. and Warnke, A. (2003) Electrophysiological investigation of the effectiveness of methylphenidate in children with and without ADHD, *Journal of Neural Transmission*, 110(7): 821–9.

Silbereisen, R.K. and Claar, A. (1982) Stimulation of social cognition in parent-child interaction: do parents make use of appropriate interaction strategies? Paper given at conference on new perspectives in the experimental study of the social development of intelligence, Geneva.

Snider, V.E. (1992) Learning styles and learning to read: a critique, *Remedial and Special Education*, 13(1): 6–18.

Sovik, N., Frostad, P. and Lie, A. (1994) Can discrepancies between IQ and basic skills be explained by learning strategies? *British Journal of Educational Psychology*, 64: 389–405.

Stahl, S.A. and Kuhn, M.R. (1995) Does whole language or instruction matched to learning styles help children learn to read? *School Psychology Review*, 24(3): 393–404.

Stenhouse, L. (1981) What counts as research? In J. Rudduck and D. Hopkins (eds) (1985) *Readings from the Work of Lawrence Stenhouse*. London: Heinemann.

Sternberg, R.J. (1997) *Thinking Styles*. Cambridge: Cambridge University Press.

Strauss, A.L. (1998) *Basics of Qualitative Research: Techniques and Procedures for Developing Grounded Theory*. Thousand Oaks, CA: Sage.

Swindells, R. (1995) *Stone Cold*. London: Puffin.

Tanner, H. and Jones, S. (1999) Scaffolding metacognition: reflective discourse and the development of mathematical thinking, paper presented at British Educational Research Association Conference, University of Sussex, Brighton.

TES (2006) Comparing child well-being in OECD countries.

Tharp, R. and Gallimore, R. (1991) A theory of teaching as assisted performance, in P. Light, S. Sheldon and M. Woodhead (eds) *Child Development in Social Context 2: Learning to Think*. Milton Keynes: Open University Press.

Thompson, P. (2006) Towards a sociocognitive model of progression in spoken English, *Cambridge Journal of Education*, 36(2): 207–20.

Tizard, B. and Hughes, M. (1991) Reflections on young children learning, in G. Walford (ed.) *Doing Educational Research*. New York: Routledge.

Tooley, J. and Darby, D. (1998) *Educational Research: A Critique: A Survey of Published Educational Research*. London: OFSTED.

Vermunt, J.D. (1998) The regulation of constructive learning processes, *British Journal of Educational Psychology*, 68: 149–71.

Vygotsky, L.S. (1934) *The Fundamentals of Pedology*. Moscow: Second Moscow Medical Institute.

Vygotsky, L.S. (1962) *Thought and Language*. New York: Wiley.

Vygotsky, L.S. (1978) *Mind in Society: The Development of Higher Psychological Processes*. Cambridge, MA: Harvard University Press.

Wade, S.E., Trathen, W. and Schraw, G. (1990) An analysis of spontaneous study strategies, *Reading Research Quarterly*, 25: 147–66.

Warr, P. and Downing, J. (2000) Learning strategies, learning anxiety and knowledge acquisition, *British Journal of Psychology*, 91: 311–33.

Waterhouse, P. (1983) *Supported Self-study in Secondary Education*. Working paper 24, London: Council for Educational Technology.

Watkins C. (1983) *Learning about Learning Enhances Performance*. Working paper 24, London: Council for Educational Technology.

Weinstein, C.E., Goetz, E.T. and Alexander, P.A. (1988) *Learning and Study Strategies: Issues in Assessment, Instruction and Evaluation*. San Diego: Academic Press.

Weinstein, C.E., Husman, J. and Dieking, D.R. (2000) Self-regulation interventions with a focus on learning strategies, in M. Bokaerts (ed.) *Handbook of Self-regulation*. New York: Academic Press.

Wellman, H.M. (1981) Metamemory revisited, paper presented at Social Research into Child Development, April 1981, Boston.

Wells, G. (1986) *The Meaning Makers*. London: Heinemann.

Wertsch, J.V. and Addison-Stone, C. (1985) The concept of internalization in Vygotsky's account of the genesis of higher mental functions, in J.V. Wertsch (ed.) *Culture, Communication and Cognition: Vygotskian Perspectives*. Cambridge: Cambridge University Press.

Wertsch, J.V. (ed.) (1985) *Culture, Communication and Cognition: Vygotskian Perspectives*. Cambridge: Cambridge University Press.

White, C. (2000) Strategies are not enough: the importance of classroom culture in the teaching of writing, *Education*, 2: 3–13.

Williams, T., Williams, K., Kastberg, D. and Jocelyn, L. (2005) Achievement and affect in OECD nations, *Oxford Review of Education*, 31(4): 517–45.

Wilson, B. (1997) Thoughts on theory in educational technology, *Educational Technology*, 97(1): 22–7.

Wilson, V. (2001) Can thinking skills be taught? www.scre.ac.uk accessed on 13 Dec. 2001.

Wittrock, M.C. (1988) A constructive review of research on learning strategies, in C.E. Weinstein, E.T. Goetz and P.A. Alexander (eds) *Learning and Study Strategies: Issues in Assessment, Instruction and Evaluation*. San Diego: Academic Press.

Wolcott, H.F. (1990) *Writing up Qualitative Research*. London: Sage.

Wood, D. (1998) *How Children Think and Learn*, 2nd edn. London: Blackwell.

Woods, P. (1990) *The Happiest Days: How Pupils Cope with School*. London: Falmer Press.

Yates, G.C.R. (2000) Applying learning style research in the classroom: some cautions and the way ahead, in R. Riding and R. Rayner (eds) *International Perspectives, Individual Differences*: vol. 1, *Cognitive Styles*. Stamford, CT: Ablex, 347–64.

Zhang, L. (2006) Does student–teacher thinking style match/mismatch matter in students' achievement? *Educational Psychology*, 26(3): 395–409.

Zimmerman, B.J. (1997) Self-efficacy and educational development, in A. Bandura *Self-efficacy: The Exercise of Control*. New York: W.H. Freeman.

Zimmerman, B.J. (2000) Attaining self-regulation: a social cognitive perspective, in M. Bokaerts (ed.) *Handbook of Self-regulation*. New York: Academic Press.

Zimmerman, B.J. and Martinez-Pons, M. (1990) Student differences in self-regulated learning: relating grade, sex, and giftedness to self-efficacy and strategy use, *Journal of Educational Psychology*, 82(1): 51–9.

Zivin, G. (1979) Removing common confusions about egocentric speech, private speech and self-regulation, in G. Zivin *The Development of Self-regulation through Private Speech*. New York: John Wiley.

Index

Locators shown in *italics* refer to figures and tables.

Related books from Open University Press

NEW LITERACIES (Second Edition)
EVERYDAY PRACTICES AND CLASSROOM LEARNING

Colin Lankshear and Michele Knobel

The important contribution that this book makes is the way in which it urges us to rethink literacy and the influential forces that are shaping new practices. So, if you already own a copy of the first edition, you need to buy the second edition; if you own neither, buy both – and if that's not possible, buy the second edition and borrow the first! Because *New Literacies: Everyday Practices and Classroom Learning* is essential reading.
Literacy Journal, Volume 41 Number 3 November 2007

The first edition of this popular book explored new literacies, new kinds of knowledge and classroom practices in the context of the massive growth of electronic information and communication technologies. This timely new edition discusses a fresh range of practices like blogging, fanfiction, mobile/wireless communications, and fan practices that remix audio and visual texts. Revised and updated throughout, the book examines:

- Popular practices and social networks associated with contemporary phenomena, Flickr and Wikipedia
- Blogging, podcasting and mobile/wireless communication practices
- Writing practices within online fanfiction and manga-anime communities
- The production of Anime-Music-Video artifacts and online multimodal 'memes'

The authors look at how digital technologies and new forms of mobile communications have been embraced by young people and integrated into their everyday lives. They argue that schools ignore some of these trends at their peril, and discuss how wireless mobility might be integrated effectively into school-based pedagogies and due attention paid to new literacies in teaching and learning.

This new edition is essential reading for undergraduates and academics within literacy studies and for policy writers working within the area of digital literacy, new technologies or ICT development within education.

Contents
What's new? – New literacies and the challenge of mindsets – 'New literacies': Concepts and practices – New literacies in everyday practice – News, views and baby's got the blues: Weblogging and mediacasting as participation – Planning pedagogy for i-mode: Learning in the age of the 'mobile net' – Memes, literacy education and classroom learning – So what?

2006   272pp
978–0–335–22010–6 (Paperback)

UNDERSTANDING THINKING; UNDERSTANDING LEARNING
A GUIDE TO THINKING SKILLS IN EDUCATION
Debra McGregor

This highly informative book provides a comprehensive guide to the teaching of thinking skills in primary and secondary education.
Learning and Teaching Update

It is now recognised that thinking skills, such as problem-solving, analysis, synthesis, creativity and evaluation, can be nurtured and developed, and education professionals can play a significant role in shaping the way that children learn and think. As a result, schools are being encouraged to make greater use of thinking skills in lessons and the general emphasis on cognition has developed considerably. This book offers a comprehensive introduction to thinking skills in education and provides detailed guidance on how teachers can support cognitive development in their classrooms.

Developing Thinking; Developing Learning discusses how thinking programmes, learning activities and teachers' pedagogy in the classroom can fundamentally affect the nature of pupils' thinking, and considers the effects of the learning environment created by peers and teachers. It compares the nature, design and outcomes of established thinking programmes used in schools and also offers practical advice for teachers wishing to develop different kinds of thinking capabilities.

This is an indispensable guide to thinking skills in schools today, and is key reading for education studies students, teachers and trainee teachers, and educational psychologists.

Contents
List of figures and tables - Acknowledgements - Introduction - What do we mean by 'thinking?' - What kind of thinking should we encourage children to do? - Thinking and learning - The nature of thinking programmes developed within a subject context - The nature of general thinking skills programmes - The nature of infusing thinking - Effectiveness of thinking programmes - Development of creative thinking - Development of critical thinking - Development of metacognition - Development of problem solving capability - Synthesising the general from the particular - Professional development to support thinking classrooms - School development to support thinking communities - References - Index.

2007 344pp
978–0–335–21780–9 (Paperback)   978–0–335–21781–6 (Hardback)